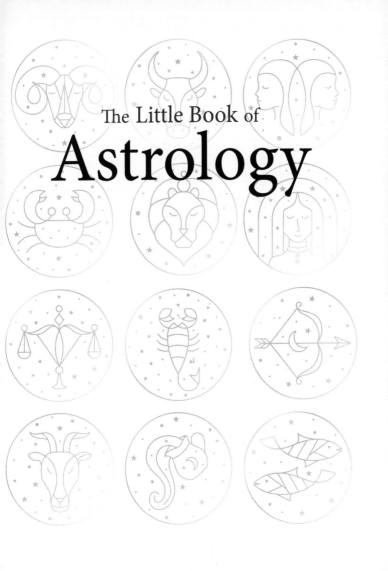

The Little Book of
Astrology

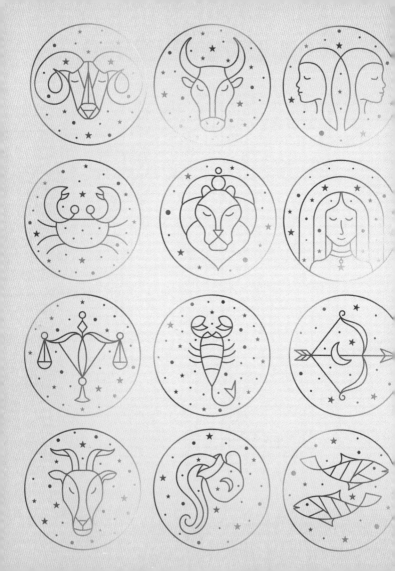

The Little Book of

Astrology

USE THE POWER OF THE PLANETS
TO REVEAL YOUR INNER DESTINY

CICO BOOKS

LONDON NEW YORK

Published in 2023 by CICO Books
An imprint of Ryland Peters & Small Ltd
20–21 Jockey's Fields   341 E 116th St
London, WC1R 4BW   New York, NY 10029

www.rylandpeters.com

10 9 8 7 6 5 4 3 2 1

A CIP catalog record for this book is available from
the Library of Congress and the British Library.

ISBN: 978 1 80065 208 8

Printed in China

Illustrator: Jacqui Mair
Illustrations on pages 1, 2, 13, 96–143:
Pixejoo—stock.adobe.com
Designer: Louise Turpin

Commissioning editor: Kristine Pidkameny
In-house editor: Jenny Dye
Art director: Sally Powell
Creative director: Leslie Harrington
Production manager: Gordana Simakovic
Publishing manager: Penny Craig

CONTENTS

Introduction

Many people think they know their astrological sign, and newspapers and magazines frequently offer daily, weekly, or monthly forecasts offering insights into our personalities and future. However, astrology is about more than simply dividing the population by twelve. The Sun is the most important planet in our birth charts, and your Sun sign is the one you will find in simple newspaper forecasts. However, your Ascendant, or Rising sign, along with the Moon, Venus, and Mars signs, all contribute to your individual astrological make-up. They add to our self-knowledge and also our understanding of other people. We each have our own unique birth chart which is determined at birth. It is a snapshot of the celestial map at the exact moment you were born. Like any map, read in the right way, it can tell us so much about where we are and where we are about to go, and can show us the myriad ways to get there.

In simple terms, the information we get from the heavenly bodies can be seen as:

The Rising sign: how you meet life

The Sun: what you think

The Moon: what you feel

Venus: what you value

Mars: how you act

Gaining insight

This book contains all the tools you need to explore your own birth chart. The book includes unique Astro wheels, simple formulas to pinpoint your Moon and Rising sign, and tables to locate your Venus and Mars signs. It is packed with information to enhance your astrological know-how. You can also use it to learn what the planets have in store and gain more control over your life. Using the positive influence of the planets, you'll be poised to grab the opportunities on offer because you will know when they are coming—just by tuning in to the prevailing planetary energy. Plotting the paths of the planets as they move through the heavens helps you decide in advance when to make those all-important decisions about love, money, and your career.

Venus and Mars on Your Lifestyle

Venus and Mars together are indicators of how you go about achieving your goals in life, and reveal what you hold dear. Mars is the masculine, extrovert expression of your personality that dictates your attitude to getting what you want in terms of money, career, and love. Venus is the feminine planet that shows you what you value, including material possessions, your lifestyle, and those you love.

The astrological glyphs for Venus and Mars are also universal feminine and masculine symbols.

Venus and Mars on Love

Venus and Mars are also astrological indicators of love and relationships, and this book will show you how their magic puts you in the right place at the right time to attract the attention you want. "Love at first sight" is not just a cliché, but something that really happens! Knowing the Moon, Venus, and Mars signs of potential lovers will give you invaluable inside information—is this latest dalliance merely a flirtation or could this be the real thing? Check out their charts to learn more about them and, more importantly, discover how to get the right response.

You may already know your Sun sign, but this book will show you how to calculate your Rising, or ascendant sign as well as your Moon, Mars, and Venus signs, and help you to use them to interpret your chart. All you need to know is your date and time of birth, and you are ready to get started.

How to Use This Book

In this book you will find astrological wheels on pages 16–19. Here's how to use them:

1 Find your Rising sign using the instructions on pages 28–29 and the table on page 29. Draw a line from your time of birth to your date of birth to do this. For example, if you were born at 2:30 P.M. on June 30, your Rising sign would be Scorpio (see below). Consult a professional astrologer if you are in any doubt. For more information on your Rising sign, see page 24.

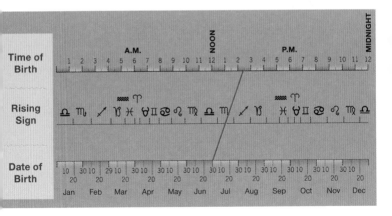

Rising signs

 Aries

 Taurus

 Gemini

 Cancer

 Leo

 Virgo

 Libra

 Scorpio

 Sagittarius

 Capricorn

 Aquarius

 Pisces

2 Find the Astro wheel on pages 16–19 which has your Rising sign aligned with the first House.

As long as you are casting a birth chart for yourself, you can refer to this wheel (with your Rising sign aligned with the 1st House). Read your personality profile for your Rising sign on pages 30–31. This adds to what you will already know from your Sun sign. See pages 26–27 for full explanations of the affairs and areas that each House holds in your life.

For example, if your Rising sign was Scorpio, find the Astro wheel on page 18 where the symbol for this sign on the inner wheel is aligned with the 1st House on the rim of the wheel as shown below. See opposite and the key on page 93 to find the glyphs and symbols for each sign.

3 Look up your Moon sign using the table on page 40. For example, the Moon sign for someone born on June 30, 1965, is Cancer. This is calculated by looking up the year and month of birth, which gives Gemini (see also below). Looking up the 30th day (see the table on page 40) gives the number 1; so count on one sign through the sequence of the zodiac (see page 93) from Gemini, which gives Cancer. Now read the profile for your sign on pages 42–43. This tells you more about the parts of your personality that you hide from others.

				JAN	FEB	MAR	APR	MAY	JUN	JUL	AUG	SEP	OCT	NOV	DEC
1927	1946	**1965**	1984	2003	Sag	Cap	Aqu	Pis	Tau	**Gem**	Leo	Vir	Sco	Sag	Aqu	Pis
1928	1947	1966	1985	2004	Ari	Gem	Gem	Leo	Vir	Sco	Sag	Aqu	Pis	Ari	Gem	Can
1929	1948	1967	1986	2005	Vir	Sco	Sco	Cap	Aqu	Pis	Tau	Gem	Leo	Vir	Lib	Sag
1930	1949	1968	1987	2006	Cap	Pis	Pis	Tau	Gem	Leo	Vir	Sco	Sag	Cap	Pis	Ari

4 Find your Moon sign on pages 94–143. For example, if your Moon sign is Cancer, find the Moon in Cancer page (see above right and page 109). On this page, and on pages 42–43 are interpretations of your Moon sign personality. This page also features advice and a prediction for the Moon's transit through the sign of Cancer, or the 4th House (see page 20).

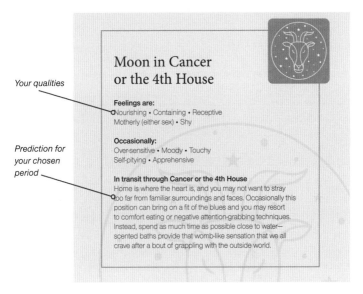

Your qualities

Moon in Cancer or the 4th House

Feelings are:
Nourishing • Containing • Receptive
Motherly (either sex) • Shy

Occasionally:
Over-sensitive • Moody • Touchy
Self-pitying • Apprehensive

Prediction for your chosen period

In transit through Cancer or the 4th House
Home is where the heart is, and you may not want to stray
too far from familiar surroundings and faces. Occasionally this
position can bring on a fit of the blues and you may resort
to comfort eating or negative attention-grabbing techniques.
Instead, spend as much time as possible close to water—
scented baths provide that womb-like sensation that we all
crave after a bout of grappling with the outside world.

5 Look up your Venus sign in the tables on pages 45–58. To do this, you only need to know your date of birth.

For example (see right), June 30, 1965 gives the Venus sign of Leo; so look up Venus in Leo on pages 60–61.

1965	
12 Jan–4 Feb	Capricorn
5–28/29 Feb	Aquarius
1–24 Mar	Pisces
25 Mar–17 Apr	Aries
18 Apr–11 May	Taurus
12 May–5 June	Gemini
6–29 June	Cancer
30 June–14 July	**Leo**
15 July–18 Aug	Virgo
19 Aug–12 Sept	Libra
13 Sept–8 Oct	Scorpio
9 Oct–4 Nov	Sagittarius
5 Nov–6 Dec	Capricorn
7 Dec–5 Feb 1966	Aquarius

6 From pages 94–143, find your Venus sign. As with the Moon sign profile, the Venus profile presents your Venusian qualities, plus a prediction.

7 Look up your Mars sign in the tables on pages 64–71. For example, June 30, 1965 gives the Mars sign of Libra; so look up Mars in Libra on pages 72–73 for an interpretation.

1965	
29 June–19 Aug	**Libra**
20 Aug–3 Oct	Scorpio
4 Oct–13 Nov	Sagittarius
14 Nov–22 Dec	Capricorn
23 Dec–29 Jan 1966	Aquarius

8 Find your Mars sign on pages 94–143. Here, you'll read your Martian qualities, plus a future prediction for Mars in this sign or House.

9 Note down where your Moon, Venus, Mars, and Sun signs fall on your Astro wheel on pages 16–19, on the outside of the wheel next to their corresponding signs. For example, if your Venus sign is Leo, write down "Venus" next to Leo on your Astro wheel. Repeat this for each of your signs. Now you have a miniature map of the heavens for when you were born. Simply read the character profiles within this book. You can repeat this process for every chart you want to explore.

Interpreting the Patterns of the Planets

Are your Venus, Sun, Mars, and Moon signs equally spaced around the wheel, or do you have clusters occupying the same House, or Houses that are close to one another? Do some fall opposite one another on the wheel? Astrology is influenced by polarity, so signs falling in one House also have an influence on the opposite House and its meaning— in simple terms, this means there's an effect on a House where you may not have any signs.

Two or three planets in one sign—intensity about the issues of this House and its opposite. Need to develop perspective.

All the planets on adjacent houses—scattered energy, a need to focus.

Planets that fall opposite each other—a need to develop compromise and cooperation if Sun or Mars. If Venus or Moon—stand up for yourself!

Planets that fall three signs apart at right angles to each other—this is challenging, and you may have dilemmas to solve. But it does produce spectacular results.

Planets that fall either two or four signs apart—complementary energies, and life runs smoothly. You need to manufacture your own goals and challenges.

Most planets below the Rising sign or the 7th House cusp—can be introspective. Learn to seek advice.

Most planets above the Rising sign or the 7th House cusp—develop self-confidence.

Most planets falling in houses 10–3 inclusive—learn to go with the flow.

Most planets falling in houses 4–9 inclusive—learn to take control.

To help you interpret the pattern of your signs at a glance, see the panel above. Now look at which Houses on the outer wheel your Venus, Sun, Mars, and Moon signs fall into. For further insight, look up the individual meanings of the signs in the Houses in chapters 2–6 and pages 94–143. For example, if you have Mars in Libra in the 12th House on your Astro wheel, after reading Mars in Libra (the 7th House) on pages 73 and 123, read Mars in Pisces (the 12th House) on page 73 and 143 for extra insight.

Astro Wheels

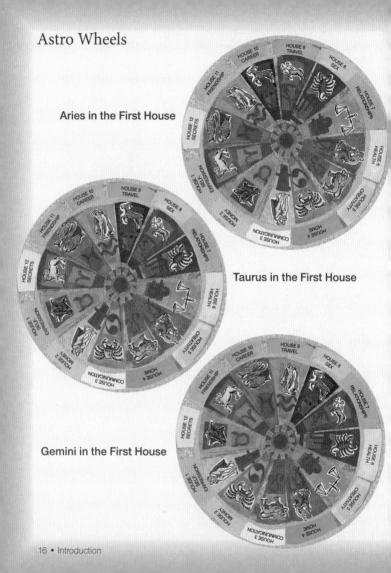

Aries in the First House

Taurus in the First House

Gemini in the First House

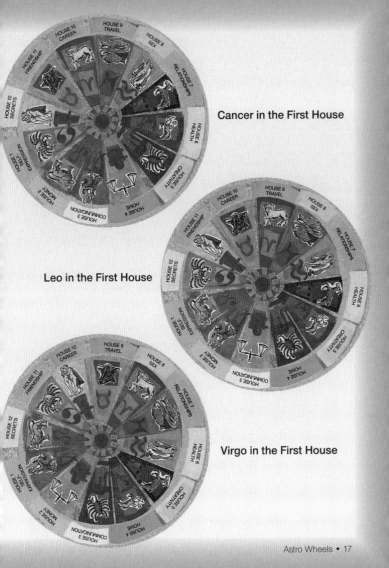

Cancer in the First House

Leo in the First House

Virgo in the First House

Libra in the First House

Scorpio in the First House

Sagittarius in the First House

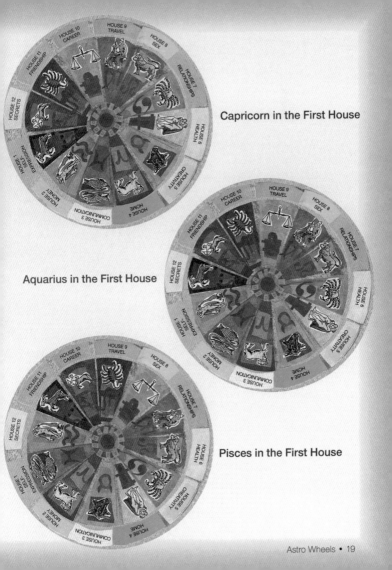

Capricorn in the First House

Aquarius in the First House

Pisces in the First House

1 Getting Started
Planets, Elements, and Houses

Your birth chart is a symbolic representation of your personality, embodying all the traits and contradictions that combine to make you unique. So understanding your chart really can be the key to greater self-knowledge and understanding. The chart consists of signs, planets, and Houses, and the relationships between them. When you first look at your chart it can seem rather complex, but all you need is to understand a few key terms and how they affect your chart.

Your birth chart will have planets in different signs (or Houses), elements, and modes. Houses occupied by planets can indicate your priorities and motivation. For example, when you use the Astro wheel and pages 9–14 in this book to create your birth chart, you can instantly see which Houses, or signs, your Sun, Moon, Venus, and Mars occupy. Together, their interpretations give you a simple birth chart. The movements of the planets are known as transits.

The Houses

The Houses represent areas of life, and the sign on the edge, or cusp, of these Houses indicates your attitude to the affairs of each House. For example, if you have the sign of Sagittarius on the cusp of your 6th House, which represents routine and health, you are more likely to leave the dirty dishes until later than if you had diligent Virgo in that place. Houses 1 to 6 concern issues related to you, and Houses 7 to 12 are linked with your relationship to others. The sign on the cusp of each House indicates the style in which you approach the affairs of that House. Each House is also associated with a zodiac sign: Aries with the first House, Taurus with the second House, Gemini with the third House, and so on. The affairs of each House are in keeping with the sign to which they correspond.

THE PLANETS

The planets signify specific human principles, and their aspects are the connections they make with each other. These connections are constantly shifting, and can have a profound effect on how you are feeling at a particular time. For example, when your Sun sign is in proud Leo, and Mars is in forthright Aries, you know what you want and how to get it. However, if your Sun sign is in conservative Taurus, and Mars is in carefree Gemini, you may feel torn between stability and change.

Venus

Mars

Sun

Moon

The Elements

The zodiac signs also have their own elements. The four elements are Fire, Earth, Air, and Water.

FIRE is spontaneous and inspired. Often optimistic, it can find practicalities daunting.

EARTH is constructive, reliable, and sensual. It understands the material world but can be over-possessive.

AIR is thoughtful and fascinated by exchanging ideas, but sometimes baffled by emotions.

WATER is at home with feelings and is sympathetic and imaginative, but occasionally needs to be reminded of reality.

The sign of Cancer, symbolized by the Crab, is associated with the element of Water.

The Modes

Each sign also has one of three modes: Cardinal, Fixed, or Mutable. The modes qualify the signs by describing how we react to the people and events around us.

CARDINAL signs can be quick to act. Initiating projects is fun, but the follow-through is a bore.

FIXED signs enjoy stability and can be resistant to change.

MUTABLE signs adapt but can find decision-making tricky.

Plus or Minus?

Signs can also be described as positive or negative—see the table opposite of zodiac signs with their elements, modes, and positive or negative attribute. Signs that share the same mode and expression but differ in element are said to be in opposition—in the table on page 23, for example, Aries and Libra are opposite Fire and Air signs.

Opposite signs tend to complement one another, and each can supply qualities that the other lacks. For example, the signs numbered 1–6 react to events personally, whereas those numbered 7–12 tend to see the bigger picture. When you meet your opposite sign, you may feel an instinctive attraction to them. The downside can be that your opposite sign could be overpowering, as some qualities appear so opposite to your own. However, opposite signs can share similar values: take homely Cancer and money-making Capricorn. The emotional Crab may seem at odds with the business-minded Goat, but they both need

THE SIGNS AND THEIR QUALITIES

SIGN	ELEMENT	MODE	EXPRESSION
1 Aries	Fire	Cardinal	Positive
2 Taurus	Earth	Fixed	Negative
3 Gemini	Air	Mutable	Positive
4 Cancer	Water	Cardinal	Negative
5 Leo	Fire	Fixed	Positive
6 Virgo	Earth	Mutable	Negative
7 Libra	Air	Cardinal	Positive
8 Scorpio	Water	Fixed	Negative
9 Sagittarius	Fire	Mutable	Positive
10 Capricorn	Earth	Cardinal	Negative
11 Aquarius	Air	Fixed	Positive
12 Pisces	Water	Mutable	Negative

security and choose to achieve this in different ways. Positive Fire and Air signs tend to be extrovert and objective, while Earth and Water signs are Negative, introvert, and subjective. Remember that no sign is better than another—each has its share of light and dark characteristics.

2 Understanding Your Rising Sign
How Do You Meet Life?

Picture the zodiac as a celestial ring around the Earth. This ring is divided into the twelve astrological signs and, as the Earth makes its daily revolution, the sign that appears to be "rising" on the eastern horizon changes moment by moment. So your personal Rising sign is the sign that appeared to rise on the horizon at your moment of birth.

The Rising sign is not a planet, but it denotes the start of your birth chart, so working out your Rising sign is the first step in using this book. This will take around five minutes (see pages 28–29) using one chart. You will need your date and time of birth. Then find the Astro wheel on pages 16–19 where your Rising sign is aligned with the 1st astrological House. (In astrological terms, your Rising sign is said to be on the cusp of the 1st House). Now you will see which signs are on the cusp of each of your personal astrological Houses. This gives you insight into your feelings and attitudes to life. Opposite is an illustration of the twelve Houses and overleaf is an explanation of their meaning, so when you align your Rising sign with the 1st House you will have an instant interpretation for your signs in the Houses.

What Does a Rising Sign Reveal?

Your Rising sign reveals how you experience and impact the world around you, and it subtly complements or detracts from your Sun sign (see pages 32–37). It also qualifies your closest personal relationships. For example, if your Sun sign is Scorpio and you have Gemini Rising, you may get attention from Sagittarians. This is because Gemini is opposite Sagittarius on the zodiac wheel and opposites often attract.

If you have calculated your Rising sign and the interpretation feels inaccurate, read through the signs before and after to see which characteristics most fit your personality, as there is always a margin of error when using a quick-finder method rather than consulting a qualified astrologer. If you do not know your time of birth, you can also ask a friend to read the profiles and see which applies best to you. However, in the long-term, do try to trace your exact time of birth.

The astrological Houses

The inner wheel shows the signs of the zodiac by their glyphs and symbols. The outer ring of the wheel shows the twelve astrological Houses. To begin compiling your birth chart, find the Astro wheel on pages 16–19 that has your Rising sign aligned with the 1st House on the outer wheel.

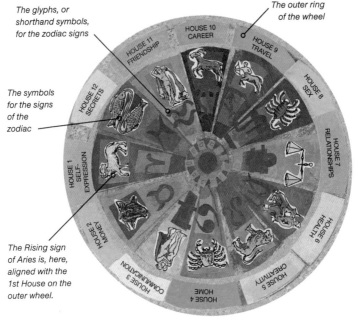

The glyphs, or shorthand symbols, for the zodiac signs

The outer ring of the wheel

The symbols for the signs of the zodiac

The Rising sign of Aries is, here, aligned with the 1st House on the outer wheel.

The Attributes of the Houses
Where's the Action?

Each astrological House represents twelve different aspects of life:
Houses 1 to 6 represent personal issues, while Houses 7 to 12 reflect
your relationship to other people and the broader world. The sign on the
cusp of each House indicates the style in which you approach the affairs
of that House. Don't worry if there are no planets in the Houses—it doesn't
mean that nothing is happening there. Each House is visited in turn by the
planets during the year, highlighting the House and its concerns.

- **The 1st House: Self-expression**
  Your physical appearance, your self-image, the first impressions you make,
  and your approach to life are linked to the Ascendant and 1st House. It can
  describe the atmosphere around your birth and upbringing.
- **The 2nd House: Money**
  Personal talent and resources are linked to this House, which rules
  possessions and earnings and how you feel about them. It separates what
  is yours from what you share with others. The sign on the cusp indicates
  what you value most.
- **The 3rd House: Communication**
  Immediate communication is highlighted here. This House rules
  relationships with siblings, schooling, neighbors, your environment, and
  short journeys. TV, writing, or an affinity with the media are concerns too.
- **The 4th House: Home**
  This is the House of the home—literally and symbolically. Look at the sign
  on the cusp to see how you find security. This connects to your inheritance
  via your father. Planets here can describe him.
- **The 5th House: Creativity**
  Creativity and self-expression are keynotes. It describes your attitude to love
  affairs, children, and amusement. Transits here encourage you to take a
  risk—it often pays off.

- **The 6th House: Health**
  Your day-to-day routine and how you fit in at work are 6th-House issues. It explains how you go about your chores and responsibilities. Your health also comes under scrutiny as does your attitude to wellbeing. Pets are linked to the 6th House.
- **The 7th House: Relationships**
  Opposite the 1st, this House describes how you experience others. How competitive or cooperative you are depends on the sign on the cusp. The House rules committed relationships such as cohabitation and marriage as well as business or creative ventures.
- **The 8th House: Sex**
  This is where it gets serious! The deep-level sharing of sexual commitment is symbolized here. Business partnerships involving joint finances are ruled by the 8th. Don't forget that debts also count as shared, as they represent other people's money.
- **The 9th House: Travel**
  Here, you'll discover your philosophy, including your experience of God. Higher education, orthodox religion, and professions such as the law are key concerns of this House. It also rules long journeys and foreign cultures.
- **The 10th House: Career**
  Opposite the 4th, this House rules your mother's influence and can describe her. Your attitude to authority may depend upon which sign is on the cusp. Ambition, status, and career are boosted by transits here.
- **The 11th House: Friendships**
  This is where you get involved with friends and colleagues and find whether you are a leader or one of a gang. It encompasses socializing as well as social and political activism and professional projects. Long-term goals are influenced by planets here.
- **The 12th House: Secrets**
  Traditionally the House of hidden enemies, look at planets here to see patterns that can sabotage your efforts. The 12th rules spirituality, devotion, and intuition. This House links you to the collective consciousness.

How to Find Your Rising Sign

Consulting a professional astrologer is the way to be absolutely certain of your Rising sign, but there is a quick-finder method. The table below is for Greenwich Mean Time (GMT) so depending on where you were born, you must add or deduct the number of hours either behind or ahead of GMT. For example, if you were born in New York at 3 P.M., you must add 5 hours to your birth time, and you would look at 8 P.M. on the table. If you were born in England during the summer, subtract 1 hour to allow for British Summer Time. However, during some British summers Double Summer Time was in effect. If you were born in Britain during the summers of 1941–1945 or 1947, deduct 2 hours from your time of birth. If you were born during American Summer Time in the US, deduct the number of hours ahead of normal time from your time of birth. Wherever you were born, see if a local summer time affected the clocks, and convert your time of birth to GMT.

Example: If you were born in New York on November 10 at 6 P.M., convert this to GMT i.e. 11 P.M., mark this on the top and bottom lines, and join the marks as shown in red. The line passes through Leo, your Rising sign.

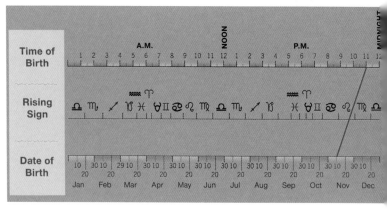

STEP 1 Mark your time of birth on the top line.
STEP 2 Mark the day and month of your birth.
STEP 3 Join the two marks. Where they cross the middle line or upper middle line, you will find the symbol for your Rising sign.

Rising sign finder
Below is a blank Rising sign finder so you can calculate your own Rising sign.

Tip: When you're calculating your own Rising sign, remember to add or subtract hours from birth times if you were a summer baby.

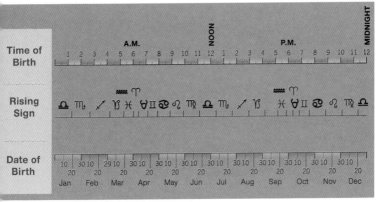

What Your Rising Sign Means

 Aries Rising Meeting life head on, you go for your goals and brush aside obstacles, human or otherwise.

 Taurus Rising Happiest in the world of the senses, you prefer a peaceful life. Surprises unsettle you, and sometimes you can't let go.

 Gemini Rising Life is an endless parade of new and enthralling opportunities, but you might learn more if you look beneath the surface.

 Cancer Rising Intuitive and receptive, your indirect approach may confuse, but you are surprisingly effective.

 Leo Rising Me first! So strong-willed, you are mainly interested in the effect you have on others. Remember, everyone needs attention.

 Virgo Rising Why are you so hard on yourself? You deserve emotional contentment and material success as well.

Libra Rising Decisions are your challenge. You can't please everyone all of the time, so learn to please yourself instead.

Scorpio Rising Oozing mystery and magnetism, keeping secrets is your hobby. But not everyone has something to hide!

Sagittarius Rising Always looking for the next challenge (or the next affair), you can get lost in your overly adventurous vision of the future.

Capricorn Rising Allow a tiny chink to appear in your armor, and let others appreciate your generous and practical approach to life.

Aquarius Rising Your whole approach is governed by your ideals. Remember, idealism is only virtuous when tempered with compassion.

Pisces Rising Straight-jacketing yourself is a recipe for confusion. You're capable of unconditional love—so learn to love yourself.

3 Understanding the Sun
What is Your Aim in Life?

Human existence would cease without the Sun's life-giving energy, and likewise your own Sun is the hub around which the other planets wheel and spin.

   The force of the Sun provides your motivation and drive. Astrological forecasts in newspapers and magazines are usually based on Sun signs alone, as they describe the outward, or most immediately obvious effects of the position of the Sun through the zodiac signs or Houses.

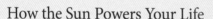

How the Sun Powers Your Life

In terms of relationships, the Sun's masculine energy symbolizes your father or a father-figure and other significant men in your life, just as the Moon is linked with mothers and women in general. The Sun also symbolizes your ego and how you affirm your identity and individuality. The impetus to express and exert your free will is powered by the Sun in your chart. As your life unfolds, so does your understanding and appreciation of your own Sun-sign qualities.

   In contrast to the more insular, backward-looking Moon, the Sun is goal- and future-oriented, and is linked to personal and public aims and ambitions. The interdependent energies of the Sun and Moon—one male, one female—can be likened to yin and yang.

The colors orange and yellow, the marigold flower,
and the peacock are associated with the Sun.

The Sun in the Signs and Houses

Aries *March 21–April 20*

No shrinking violet, you're very single-minded and direct in all your dealings with others. While faster is not necessarily better, however, you do tend to succeed, conquering more mountains than most.

The 1st House

This House is where you make an impact and you have both the will and individuality to forge your own path through life. Getting your own way come naturally to you, but be aware that sometimes you don't even notice that others might want to have their say.

Taurus *April 21–May 21*

For Taureans, patience is your secret weapon in your quest for emotional and material security. A life of sensuous luxury—get that and you're already in heaven.

The 2nd House

Developing your own unique talent is how you obtain the material security that you need. Remember that possessions are only part of the equation— real confidence comes from self-knowledge. Look at your Sun sign to understand what you value the most.

Gemini *May 22–June 21*

Your thirst for knowledge is always in overdrive. However, making sense of all that information is a job for someone else! You are passionate about new acquaintances and interests, but you leave a trail of unfinished business in your wake.

The 3rd House

With the Sun in the 3rd House, you are very proud of your mind. Sometimes, you get so excited about a new skill or passion that you just have to let everyone know. Early on in life, you may find that you have the most fun with your siblings—later, your local neighborhood is your favorite place.

Cancer *June 22–July 23*

You appreciate the past, but the nostalgic Cancerian often wants to linger there, avoiding the here-and-now. Resist the temptation and stay in the present. Your warm and caring nature also means you tend to mother everyone with kindness, but any hint of rejection makes for a moody Crab.

The 4th House

Emotional security is crucial for you, so establishing your own home may be an early goal. Your family inheritance makes a big impression, although you may often struggle against it. Sometimes you find yourself resorting to childhood treats when you need a little comfort.

Leo *July 24–August 23*

Trying every ride in life's magical theme-park is your goal and self-expression is the key. Nothing cramps your style more than a list of "should"s.

The 5th House

You need an outlet for your creative spirit. You may not be a genius, but you revel in your creations. Occasionally child-like, you have an affinity with children. If anyone can turn life into a game, it's you.

Virgo *August 24–September 23*

The perfection you seek is all in your head. Put down the self-help manuals and take time out to gaze at the sunset now and again. It's not selfish to nurture yourself.

The 6th House

You need a routine to feel happy and secure, otherwise you can feel all at sea. Health matters to you and you're often the first to try that new fitness club. Pleasure comes from a job well done and close relationships at work.

Libra *September 24–October 23*

You may feel that you're here to bring peace, love, and understanding to the world—the balance and harmony symbolized by the Libran scales. However, don't ignore reality.

The 7th House

You meet yourself when you meet others. Going it alone is not your style and you may make relationships your goal. Sometimes your accommodating nature means that you feel unloved. Make a stand for independence—others will soon agree with you.

Scorpio *October 24–November 22*

Aware of what can't be seen, you resonate with life's mystery. Transformation is your objective, and superficiality appalls you. Learn to accept what you can't control.

The 8th House

Positively, every experience can be a lesson learned. You understand the true meaning of sharing which is why you are picky about who meets the real you. They must prove their worth first. You could be a canny financial operator if you put your mind to it.

Sagittarius *November 23–December 21*

You have your eyes set on the horizon, but your feet are on the ground; the meaning of life is your goal. The journey, not the destination is what excites you. Although it's boring, attention to detail ultimately pays off.

The 9th House

Retaining your idealism is your life's work. Any knocks along the way only serve to fuel your obsessive search for knowledge. You always have the big picture in mind, so much so that you can occasionally stumble over the details.

Capricorn *December 22–January 20*
You may crave material success, but your integrity is your most prized possession. Lighten up—others are not as demanding.

The 10th House
The 10th House is the House of ambition—your Sun sign gives you the clue as to where yours may lie. Remember that there is room for relationships in your life as you climb that slippery ladder of success. It may take time but you always reach your goal.

Aquarius *January 21–February 19*
Reforming anything, large or small, inspires you. Remember, cooperation is your ally, but fanaticism is your enemy.

The 11th House
Where you lead, others usually follow. Your enthusiasm for your pet projects enables you to inspire others. You think nothing of working all day followed by a night out.

Pisces *February 20–March 20*
We may all be a part of the greater whole, but never forget that you are an individual as well. Satisfaction may come from working with the needy—just don't take them home.

The 12th House
You can tune in to the collective mood and you have a gift for spotting trends. You could make professional use of this, but you hate to be pushy. You may find your niche in the healing arts where your talents are valued.

4 Understanding the Moon
How Do You Feel?

The mysterious Moon balances and complements the Sun, reflecting the Sun's light rather than giving off any of her own. The Moon is a feminine symbol, representing fertility, your mother, and women in general, and domesticity. She describes how you express your feelings. Your own Moon sign can also indicate your physical appearance and your general state of health—see the Moon sign profiles on pages 42–43.

Traditionally, water symbolizes the emotions, and the Moon is intrinsically linked with this primal element, causing the ebb and flow of the tides. As the Moon influences the seas and rivers of the planet, so she affects the water and other fluids within the body—after all, we comprise 90 per cent water. At the beck and call of the Moon, our response to her movement in the firmament causes us to react, whereas the forthright, masculine Sun denotes direct and outward action.

Private Moon, Public Sun?

The Moon shows how you behave in private, so compatible Moons are essential for domestic harmony. What you like to eat, how you choose to relax, and what makes you feel secure all come under her influence.

However, like the active Sun, the Moon does have her own outgoing qualities. Because her focus is on relating to oneself and interacting with others, the desire to serve and connect with other people takes her influence beyond the private world of the emotions to the public domain. Therefore, your Moon sign may also indicate how you subtly respond to others in a work, as well as a family, environment.

The Moon is also linked to the past. As the Sun goes forward into the future, the Moon looks to factual history or sentimental nostalgia depending on the sign, or House, in which the Moon falls in a birth chart.

The Moon is associated with fertility, milk, motherhood, and water.

How to Find Your Moon Sign

The Moon travels through the entire zodiac each month, only staying in one sign for a couple of days. In the table opposite, find your birth year on the left and read across to your birth month column on the right; note the sign. Now look at the table below and find your birth date. Underneath is a number from 0 to 12. Count that number on from that sign to find your Moon sign. For example, if your birth date is February 9, 1978, first find 1978. Read across until you get to February, where you'll find Scorpio. Look up your birth date, 9, below. Under the number 9 is 4, so count on 4 signs from Scorpio in the standard zodiac sequence (see page 93) to reach Pisces, which is your Moon sign. Remember that this is astro-professional's shorthand. If you feel that the Moon sign is wrong for you, read the signs before and after to see if either sign fits your personality better.

DATE OF BIRTH

1st	2nd	3rd	4th	5th	6th	7th	8th
0	1	1	1	2	2	3	3

9th	10th	11th	12th	13th	14th	15th	16th
4	4	5	5	5	6	6	7

17th	18th	19th	20th	21st	22nd	23rd	24th
7	8	8	9	9	10	10	10

25th	26th	27th	28th	29th	30th	31st
11	11	12	12	1	1	1

Year of Birth	Month of Birth											
	JAN	FEB	MAR	APR	MAY	JUN	JUL	AUG	SEP	OCT	NOV	DEC
1920 1939 1958 1977 1996	Tau	Can	Can	Vir	Lib	Sag	Cap	Aqu	Ari	Tau	Can	Leo
1921 1940 1959 1978 1997	Lib	Sco	Sag	Cap	Aqu	Ari	Tau	Can	Leo	Vir	Sco	Sag
1922 1941 1960 1979 1998	Aqu	Ari	Ari	Gem	Can	Leo	Vir	Sco	Cap	Aqu	Ari	Tau
1923 1942 1961 1980 1999	Gem	Leo	Leo	Lib	Sco	Cap	Aqu	Ari	Tau	Gem	Leo	Vir
1924 1943 1962 1981 2000	Sco	Sag	Cap	Aqu	Ari	Tau	Gem	Leo	Lib	Sco	Sag	Cap
1925 1944 1963 1982 2001	Pis	Tau	Tau	Can	Leo	Lib	Sco	Sag	Aqu	Pis	Tau	Gem
1926 1945 1964 1983 2002	Leo	Vir	Lib	Sco	Sag	Aqu	Pis	Tau	Can	Leo	Vir	Lib
1927 1946 1965 1984 2003	Sag	Cap	Aqu	Pis	Tau	Gem	Leo	Vir	Sco	Sag	Aqu	Pis
1928 1947 1966 1985 2004	Ari	Gem	Gem	Leo	Vir	Sco	Sag	Aqu	Pis	Ari	Gem	Can
1929 1948 1967 1986 2005	Vir	Sco	Sco	Cap	Aqu	Pis	Tau	Gem	Leo	Vir	Lib	Sag
1930 1949 1968 1987 2006	Cap	Pis	Pis	Tau	Gem	Leo	Vir	Sco	Sag	Cap	Pis	Ari
1931 1950 1969 1988 2007	Tau	Can	Can	Vir	Lib	Sag	Cap	Pis	Ari	Gem	Can	Leo
1932 1951 1970 1989 2008	Lib	Sag	Sag	Aqu	Pis	Tau	Gem	Can	Vir	Lib	Sag	Cap
1933 1952 1971 1990 2009	Pis	Ari	Tau	Gem	Can	Vir	Lib	Sag	Cap	Aqu	Ari	Tau
1934 1953 1972 1991 2010	Can	Vir	Vir	Lib	Sag	Cap	Pis	Ari	Gem	Can	Vir	Lib
1935 1954 1973 1992	Sco	Cap	Cap	Pis	Ari	Gem	Can	Vir	Sco	Sag	Cap	Aqu
1936 1955 1974 1993	Ari	Tau	Gem	Leo	Vir	Lib	Sco	Cap	Pis	Ari	Tau	Can
1937 1956 1975 1994	Leo	Lib	Lib	Sag	Cap	Pis	Ari	Tau	Can	Leo	Lib	Sco
1938 1957 1976 1995	Cap	Aqu	Pis	Ari	Tau	Can	Leo	Lib	Sco	Cap	Aqu	Ari

The Moon in the Signs and Houses

Aries or the 1st House
You can be quick to take offense but you are definitely the sort of person who pulls themselves together regardless. Your feelings are easily aroused, especially if your independence is threatened.

Taurus or the 2nd House
Laid back, nurturing, and tender, you're a welcome support to others. You love your home comforts and know the value of a hot meal and a back-rub.

Gemini or the 3rd House
Feelings are something you'd rather not think about––you can't take them apart and see how they work. As long as no one takes away your telephone, you're happy.

Cancer or the 4th House
A shoulder to cry on? You bet! Emotionally intuitive, you like nothing more than to gather your nearest and dearest around you. However, you are so sensitive that letting go of past hurt is another matter entirely.

Leo or the 5th House
You're not really a self-centered personality, but some attention certainly puts the smile back on your face. Being sidelined or overlooked results in a big sulk.

Virgo or the 6th House
Emotional security depends upon how much you feel needed by others. If you have too little to do, you could be a case study for hypochondria.

Libra or the 7th House

Above all, you need a life partner, and the thought of being left out and alone terrifies you. While you'll do anything to avoid conflict with others, remember that sometimes feelings need to be aired so progress can continue.

Scorpio or the 8th House

If your Moon is in secretive Scorpio, then you may hide your passionate feelings to such an extent that you have elevated it to an art form. Your feelings run very deep, however, and you can make a grievance last a lifetime.

Sagittarius or the 9th House

Your emotional honesty naturally endears you to some people, yet has other sensitive souls running for the hills. Given the Sagittarian need for freedom and travel, any kind of restriction makes you feel claustrophobic and panicky.

Capricorn or the 10th House

You may have learned self-discipline, rather than self-love, at your mother's knee. Give yourself permission to relax; and don't be quite so hard on yourself.

Aquarius or the 11th House

You're friendly in the extreme, but fear of intimacy means you are better at understanding society's pain than your own feelings.

Pisces or the 12th House

Intuitively picking up on collective emotions, you may have trouble separating your own. Periods of solitude help to heal.

5 Understanding Venus
What Do You Value?

Venus can purr like a kitten or roar like a lion. Venus rules beauty, taste, attraction, money, and, in the wider sense, your value system. She describes what you find attractive and what you bring to your day-to-day relationships as well as your most intimate liaisons. Look at Venus to see how you approach cooperation and sharing. In a man's chart, her qualities represent his dream girl. In a woman's chart, it describes her particular brand of seduction. Venus also relates to your personal wealth and value in terms of the possessions, goods, and money that you have. Venus is close to the Sun, so it is often found in the same sign as the Sun or in a sign close by. Venus appears to accelerate, move ahead of the Sun, then halt and go backwards for a while before moving forward once again.

In the tables on the following pages, look up your date of birth and read across to discover your Venus sign. For fun, try the quiz on page 59 to see where you stand before you consider your Mars aspects.

The rose and apple represent the femininity and fertility of Venus, and the grapes her love of luxury and comfort.

1935

–7 Jan	Capricorn
8–31 Jan	Aquarius
1–25 Feb	Pisces
26 Feb–21 Mar	Aries
22 Mar–15 Apr	Taurus
16 Apr–10 May	Gemini
11 May–6 June	Cancer
7 June–6 July	Leo
7 July–8 Nov	Virgo
9 Nov–7 Dec	Libra
8 Dec–2 Jan 1936	Scorpio

1936

3–27 Jan	Sagittarius
28 Jan–21 Feb	Capricorn
22 Feb–16 Mar	Aquarius
17 Mar–10 Apr	Pisces
11 Apr–4 May	Aries
5–28 May	Taurus
29 May–22 June	Gemini
23 June–16 July	Cancer
17 July–10 Aug	Leo
11 Aug–3 Sept	Virgo
4–27 Sept	Libra
28 Sept–22 Oct	Scorpio
23 Oct–15 Nov	Sagittarius
16 Nov–10 Dec	Capricorn
11 Dec–5 Jan 1937	Aquarius

1937

6 Jan–1 Feb	Pisces
2 Feb–8 Mar	Aries
9 Mar–13 Apr	Taurus
14 Apr–3 June	Aries
4 June–6 July	Taurus
7 July–3 Aug	Gemini
4–30 Aug	Cancer
31 Aug–24 Sept	Leo
25 Sept–18 Oct	Virgo
19 Oct–11 Nov	Libra

12 Nov–5 Dec	Scorpio
6–29 Dec	Sagittarius
30 Dec–22 Jan 1938	Capricorn

1938

23 Jan–15 Feb	Aquarius
16 Feb–11 Mar	Pisces
12 Mar–4 Apr	Aries
5–28 Apr	Taurus
29 Apr–23 May	Gemini
24 May–17 June	Cancer
18 June–13 July	Leo
14 July–8 Aug	Virgo
9 Aug–6 Sept	Libra
7 Sept–12 Oct	Scorpio
13 Oct–14 Nov	Sagittarius
15 Nov–3 Jan 1939	Scorpio

1939

4 Jan–5 Feb	Sagittarius
6 Feb–4 Mar	Capricorn
5–30 Mar	Aquarius
31 Mar–24 Apr	Pisces
25 Apr–19 May	Aries
20 May–13 June	Taurus
14 June–8 July	Gemini
9 July–1 Aug	Cancer
2–25 Aug	Leo
26 Aug–19 Sept	Virgo
20 Sept–13 Oct	Libra
14 Oct–6 Nov	Scorpio
7–30 Nov	Sagittarius
1–24 Dec	Capricorn
25 Dec–18 Jan 1940	Aquarius

1940

19 Jan–12 Feb	Pisces
13 Feb–8 Mar	Aries
9 Mar–4 Apr	Taurus
5 Apr–6 May	Gemini
7 May–4 July	Cancer
5 July–1 Aug	Gemini
2 Aug–8 Sept	Cancer
9 Sept–6 Oct	Leo
7 Oct–1 Nov	Virgo
2–26 Nov	Libra
27 Nov–20 Dec	Scorpio
21 Dec–13 Jan 1941	Sagittarius

1941

14 Jan–6 Feb	Capricorn
7 Feb–2 Mar	Aquarius
3–27 Mar	Pisces
28 Mar–20 Apr	Aries
21 Apr–14 May	Taurus
15 May–7 June	Gemini
8 June–2 July	Cancer
3–27 July	Leo
28 July–21 Aug	Virgo
22 Aug–16 Sept	Libra
17 Sept–10 Oct	Scorpio
11 Oct–6 Nov	Sagittarius
7 Nov–5 Dec	Capricorn
6 Dec–6 Apr 1942	Aquarius

1942

7 Apr–6 May	Pisces
7 May–2 June	Aries
3–27 June	Taurus
28 June–23 July	Gemini
24 July–19 Aug	Cancer
18 Aug–10 Sept	Leo
11 Sept–4 Oct	Virgo
5–28 Oct	Libra
29 Oct–21 Nov	Scorpio
22 Nov–15 Dec	Sagittarius

16 Dec–8 Jan 1943	Capricorn

1943

9–31 Jan	Aquarius
1–25 Feb	Pisces
26 Feb–21 Mar	Aries
22 Mar–15 Apr	Taurus
16 Apr–11 May	Gemini
12 May–7 June	Cancer
8 June–7 July	Leo
8 July–9 Nov	Virgo
10 Nov–8 Dec	Libra
9 Dec–3 Jan 1944	Scorpio

1944

4–28 Jan	Sagittarius
29 Jan–21 Feb	Capricorn
22 Feb–17 Mar	Aquarius
18 Mar–10 Apr	Pisces
11 Apr–4 May	Aries
5–29 May	Taurus
30 May–22 June	Gemini
23 June–17 July	Cancer
18 July–10 Aug	Leo
11 Aug–3 Sept	Virgo
4–28 Sept	Libra
29 Sept–22 Oct	Scorpio
23 Oct–16 Nov	Sagittarius
17 Nov–11 Dec	Capricorn
12 Dec–5 Jan 1945	Aquarius

1945

6 Jan–2 Feb	Pisces
3 Feb–11 Mar	Aries
12 Mar–6 Apr	Taurus
7 Apr–5 June	Aries
6 June–7 July	Taurus
8 July–4 Aug	Gemini
5–30 Aug	Cancer
31 Aug–24 Sept	Leo
25 Sept–19 Oct	Virgo

20 Oct–12 Nov	Libra
13 Nov–6 Dec	Scorpio
7–30 Dec	Sagittarius
31 Dec–22 Jan 1946	Capricorn

1946
23 Jan–15 Feb	Aquarius
16 Feb–11 Mar	Pisces
12 Mar–5 Apr	Aries
6–29 Apr	Taurus
30 Apr–24 May	Gemini
25 May–18 June	Cancer
19 June–13 July	Leo
14 July–9 Aug	Virgo
10 Aug–7 Sept	Libra
8 Sept–16 Oct	Scorpio
17 Oct–7 Nov	Sagittarius
8 Nov–5 Jan 1947	Scorpio

1947
6 Jan–6 Feb	Sagittarius
7 Feb–5 Mar	Capricorn
6–30 Mar	Aquarius
31 Mar–25 Apr	Pisces
26 Apr–21 May	Aries
22 May–13 June	Taurus
14 June–8 July	Gemini
9 July–2 Aug	Cancer
3–26 Aug	Leo
27 Aug–19 Sept	Virgo
20 Sept–13 Oct	Libra
14 Oct–6 Nov	Scorpio
7–30 Nov	Sagittarius
1–24 Dec	Capricorn
25 Dec–17 Jan 1948	Aquarius

1948
18 Jan–11 Feb	Pisces
12 Feb–8 Mar	Aries
9 Mar–4 Apr	Taurus
5 Apr–7 May	Gemini
8 May–29 June	Cancer
30 June–3 Aug	Gemini
4 Aug–8 Sept	Cancer
9 Sept–6 Oct	Leo
7 Oct–1 Nov	Virgo
2–26 Nov	Libra
27 Nov–20 Dec	Scorpio
21 Dec–14 Jan 1949	Sagittarius

1949
15 Jan–6 Feb	Capricorn
7 Feb–2 Mar	Aquarius
3 Mar–26 Mar	Pisces
27 Mar–19 Apr	Aries
20 Apr–13 May	Taurus
14 May–7 June	Gemini
8 June–1 July	Cancer
2–26 July	Leo
27 July–20 Aug	Virgo
21 Aug–14 Sep	Libra
15 Sep–10 Oct	Scorpio
11 Oct–6 Nov	Sagittarius
7 Nov–6 Dec	Capricorn
7 Dec–5 Apr 1950	Aquarius

1950
6 Apr–4 May	Pisces
5–31 May	Aries
1–26 June	Taurus
27 June–21 July	Gemini
22 July–15 Aug	Cancer
16 Aug–9 Sep	Leo
10 Sep–3 Oct	Virgo
4–27 Oct	Libra
28 Oct–20 Nov	Scorpio
21 Nov–13 Dec	Sagittarius
14 Dec– 6 Jan 1951	Capricorn

1951

7–30 Jan	Aquarius
31 Jan–23 Feb	Pisces
24 Feb–20 Mar	Aries
21 Mar–14 Apr	Taurus
15 Apr–10 May	Gemini
11 May–7 June	Cancer
8 June–8 July	Leo
9 July–8 Nov	Virgo
9 Nov–7 Dec	Libra
8 Dec–1 Jan 1952	Scorpio

1952

2–26 Jan	Sagittarius
27 Jan–20 Feb	Capricorn
21 Feb–15 Mar	Aquarius
16 Mar–8 Apr	Pisces
9 Apr–3 May	Aries
4–27 May	Taurus
28 May–21 June	Gemini
22 June–15 July	Cancer
16 July–8 Aug	Leo
9 Aug–2 Sep	Virgo
3–26 Sep	Libra
27 Sep–21 Oct	Scorpio
22 Oct–14 Nov	Sagittarius
15 Nov–9 Dec	Capricorn
10 Dec–4 Jan 1953	Aquarius

1953

5 Jan–1 Feb	Pisces
2 Feb–13 Mar	Aries
14–30 Mar	Taurus
31 Mar–4 June	Aries
5 June–6 July	Taurus
7 July–3 Aug	Gemini
4–29 Aug	Cancer
30 Aug–23 Sep	Leo
24 Sep–17 Oct	Virgo
18 Oct–10 Nov	Libra
11 Nov–4 Dec	Scorpio

5–28 Dec	Sagittarius
29 Dec–21 Jan 1954	Capricorn

1954

22 Jan–14 Feb	Aquarius
15 Feb–10 Mar	Pisces
11 Mar–3 Apr	Aries
4–27 Apr	Taurus
28 Apr–22 May	Gemini
23 May–16 June	Cancer
17 June–12 July	Leo
13 July–8 Aug	Virgo
9 Aug–5 Sep	Libra
6 Sep–22 Oct	Scorpio
23–26 Oct	Sagittarius
27 Oct–5 Jan 1955	Scorpio

1955

6 Jan–5 Feb	Sagittarius
6 Feb–3 Mar	Capricorn
4–29 Mar	Aquarius
30 Mar–23 Apr	Pisces
24 Apr–18 May	Aries
19 May–12 June	Taurus
13 June–7 July	Gemini
8–31 July	Cancer
1–24 Aug	Leo
25 Aug–17 Sept	Virgo
18 Sept–12 Oct	Libra
13 Oct–5 Nov	Scorpio
6–29 Nov	Sagittarius
30 Nov–23 Dec	Capricorn
24 Dec–16 Jan 1956	Aquarius

1956

17 Jan–10 Feb	Pisces
11 Feb–6 Mar	Aries
7 Mar–3 Apr	Taurus
4 Apr–7 May	Gemini
8 May–22 June	Cancer
23 June–3 Aug	Gemini

4 Aug–7 Sept	Cancer
8 Sept–5 Oct	Leo
6–30 Oct	Virgo
31 Oct–24 Nov	Libra
25 Nov–18 Dec	Scorpio
19 Dec–11 Jan 1957	Sagittarius

1957

12 Jan–4 Feb	Capricorn
5–28/29 Feb	Aquarius
1–24 Mar	Pisces
25 Mar–18 Apr	Aries
19 Apr–12 May	Taurus
13 May–5 June	Gemini
6–30 June	Cancer
1–25 July	Leo
26 July–19 Aug	Virgo
20 Aug–13 Sept	Libra
14 Sept–9 Oct	Scorpio
10 Oct–4 Nov	Sagittarius
5 Nov–5 Dec	Capricorn
6 Dec–5 Apr 1958	Aquarius

1958

6 Apr–4 May	Pisces
5–31 May	Aries
1–25 June	Taurus
26 June–21 July	Gemini
22 July–15 Aug	Cancer
16 Aug–8 Sept	Leo
9 Sept–2 Oct	Virgo
3–26 Oct	Libra
27 Oct–19 Nov	Scorpio
20 Nov–13 Dec	Sagittarius
14 Dec–6 Jan 1959	Capricorn

1959

7–30 Jan	Aquarius
31 Jan–23 Feb	Pisces
24 Feb–19 Mar	Aries
20 Mar–13 April	Taurus

14 Apr–9 May	Gemini
10 May–5 June	Cancer
6 June–7 July	Leo
8 July–19 Sept	Virgo
20–24 Sept	Leo
25 Sept–8 Nov	Virgo
9 Nov–6 Dec	Libra
7 Dec–1 Jan 1960	Scorpio

1960

2–26 Jan	Sagittarius
27 Jan–19 Feb	Capricorn
20 Feb–15 Mar	Aquarius
16 Mar–8 Apr	Pisces
9 Apr–2 May	Aries
3–27 May	Taurus
28 May–20 June	Gemini
21 June–15 July	Cancer
16 July–8 Aug	Leo
9 Aug–1 Sept	Virgo
2–26 Sept	Libra
27 Sept–20 Oct	Scorpio
21 Oct–14 Nov	Sagittarius
15 Nov–9 Dec	Capricorn
10 Dec–4 Jan 1961	Aquarius

1961

5 Jan–1 Feb	Pisces
2 Feb–4 June	Aries
5 June–6 July	Taurus
7 July–2 Aug	Gemini
3–28 Aug	Cancer
29 Aug–22 Sept	Leo
23 Sept–17 Oct	Virgo
18 Oct–10 Nov	Libra
11 Nov–4 Dec	Scorpio
5–28 Dec	Sagittarius
29 Dec–20 Jan 1962	Capricorn

1962

21 Jan–13 Feb	Aquarius
14 Feb–9 Mar	Pisces
10 Mar–2 Apr	Aries
3–27 Apr	Taurus
28 Apr–22 May	Gemini
23 May–16 June	Cancer
17 June–11 July	Leo
12 July–7 Aug	Virgo
8 Aug–6 Sept	Libra
7 Sept–5 Jan 1963	Scorpio

1963

6 Jan–4 Feb	Sagittarius
5 Feb–3 Mar	Capricorn
4–29 Mar	Aquarius
30 Mar–23 Apr	Pisces
24 Apr–18 May	Aries
19 May–11 June	Taurus
12 June–6 July	Gemini
7–30 July	Cancer
31 July–24 Aug	Leo
25 Aug–17 Sept	Virgo
18 Sept–11 Oct	Libra
12 Oct–4 Nov	Scorpio
5–28 Nov	Sagittarius
29 Nov–22 Dec	Capricorn
23 Dec–16 Jan 1964	Aquarius

1964

17 Jan–9 Feb	Pisces
10 Feb–6 Mar	Aries
7 Mar–3 Apr	Taurus
4 Apr–8 May	Gemini
9 May–16 June	Cancer
17 June–4 Aug	Gemini
5 Aug–7 Sept	Cancer
8 Sept–4 Oct	Leo
5–30 Oct	Virgo
31 Oct–24 Nov	Libra
25 Nov–18 Dec	Scorpio

19 Dec–11 Jan 1965	Sagittarius

1965

12 Jan–4 Feb	Capricorn
5–28/29 Feb	Aquarius
1–24 Mar	Pisces
25 Mar–17 Apr	Aries
18 Apr–11 May	Taurus
12 May–5 June	Gemini
6–29 June	Cancer
30 June–14 July	Leo
15 July–18 Aug	Virgo
19 Aug–12 Sept	Libra
13 Sept–8 Oct	Scorpio
9 Oct–4 Nov	Sagittarius
5 Nov–6 Dec	Capricorn
7 Dec–5 Feb 1966	Aquarius

1966

6–24 Feb	Capricorn
25 Feb–5 Apr	Aquarius
6 Apr–4 May	Pisces
5–30 May	Aries
31 May–26 June	Taurus
27 June–20 July	Gemini
21 July–14 Aug	Cancer
15 Aug–7 Sept	Leo
8 Sept–2 Oct	Virgo
3–26 Oct	Libra
27 Oct–19 Nov	Scorpio
20 Nov–12 Dec	Sagittarius
13 Dec–5 Jan 1967	Capricorn

1967

6–29 Jan	Aquarius
30 Jan–22 Feb	Pisces
23 Feb–9 Mar	Aries
20 Mar–13 Apr	Taurus
14 Apr–9 May	Gemini
10 May–7 June	Cancer
8 June–7 July	Leo

8 July–8 Sept	Virgo
9–30 Sept	Leo
1 Oct–8 Nov	Virgo
9 Nov–6 Dec	Libra
7–31 Dec	Scorpio

1968

1–25 Jan	Sagittarius
26 Jan–19 Feb	Capricorn
20 Feb–14 Mar	Aquarius
15 Mar–7 Apr	Pisces
8 Apr–2 May	Aries
3–26 May	Taurus
27 May–20 June	Gemini
21 June–14 July	Cancer
15 July–7 Aug	Leo
8 Aug–1 Sept	Virgo
2–25 Sept	Libra
26 Sept–20 Oct	Scorpio
21 Oct–13 Nov	Sagittarius
14 Nov–8 Dec	Capricorn
9 Dec–3 Jan 1969	Aquarius

1969

4 Jan–1 Feb	Pisces
2 Feb–5 June	Aries
6 June–5 July	Taurus
6 July–2 Aug	Gemini
3–28 Aug	Cancer
29 Aug–22 Sept	Leo
23 Sept–16 Oct	Virgo
17 Oct–9 Nov	Libra
10 Nov–13 Dec	Scorpio
14–27 Dec	Sagittarius
28 Dec–20 Jan 1970	Capricorn

1970

21 Jan–13 Feb	Aquarius
14 Feb–9 Mar	Pisces
10 Mar–2 Apr	Aries
3–26 Apr	Taurus

27 Apr–21 May	Gemini
22 May–15 June	Cancer
16 June–11 July	Leo
12 July 7–7 Aug	Virgo
8 Aug–6 Sept	Libra
7 Sept–6 Jan 1971	Scorpio

1971

7 Jan–4 Feb	Sagittarius
5 Feb–3 Mar	Capricorn
4–28 Mar	Aquarius
29 Mar–22 Apr	Pisces
23 Apr–17 May	Aries
18 May–11 June	Taurus
12 June–5 July	Gemini
6–30 July	Cancer
31 July–23 Aug	Leo
24 Aug–16 Sept	Virgo
17 Sept–10 Oct	Libra
11 Oct–4 Nov	Scorpio
5–28 Nov	Sagittarius
29 Nov–22 Dec	Capricorn
23 Dec–15 Jan 1972	Aquarius

1972

16 Jan–9 Feb	Pisces
10 Feb–6 Mar	Aries
7 Mar–3 Apr	Taurus
4 Apr–9 May	Gemini
10 May–10 June	Cancer
11 June–5 Aug	Gemini
6 Aug–6 Sept	Cancer
7 Sep–4 Oct	Leo
5–29 Oct	Virgo
30 Oct–23 Nov	Libra
24 Nov–17 Dec	Scorpio
18 Dec–10 Jan 1973	Sagittarius

1973

11 Jan–3 Feb	Capricorn
4–27 Feb	Aquarius
28 Feb–23 Mar	Pisces
24 Mar–17 Apr	Aries
18 Apr–11 May	Taurus
12 May–4 June	Gemini
5–29 June	Cancer
30 June–24 July	Leo
25 July–18 Aug	Virgo
19 Aug–12 Sept	Libra
13 Sep–8 Oct	Scorpio
9 Oct–4 Nov	Sagittarius
5 Nov–6 Dec	Capricorn
7 Dec–28 Jan 1974	Aquarius

1974

29 Jan–27 Feb	Capricorn
28 Feb–5 Apr	Aquarius
6 Apr–3 May	Pisces
4–30 May	Aries
31 May–24 June	Taurus
25 June–20 July	Gemini
21 July–13 Aug	Cancer
14 Aug–7 Sept	Leo
8 Sept–1 Oct	Virgo
2–25 Oct	Libra
26 Oct–18 Nov	Scorpio
19 Nov–12 Dec	Sagittarius
13 Dec–5 Jan 1975	Capricorn

1975

6–29 Jan	Aquarius
30 Jan–22 Feb	Pisces
23 Feb–18 Mar	Aries
19 Mar–12 Apr	Taurus
13 Apr–8 May	Gemini
9 May–5 June	Cancer
6 June–8 July	Leo
9 July–1 Sept	Virgo
2 Sept–3 Oct	Leo

4 Oct–8 Nov	Virgo
9 Nov–6 Dec	Libra
7–31 Dec	Scorpio

1976

1–25 Jan	Sagittarius
26 Jan–18 Feb	Capricorn
19 Feb–14 Mar	Aquarius
15 Mar–7 Apr	Pisces
8 Apr–1 May	Aries
2–26 May	Taurus
27 May–19 June	Gemini
20 June–13 July	Cancer
14 July–7 Aug	Leo
8–31 Aug	Virgo
1–25 Sept	Libra
26 Sept–19 Oct	Scorpio
20 Oct–13 Nov	Sagittarius
14 Nov–8 Dec	Capricorn
9 Dec–3 Jan 1977	Aquarius

1977

4 Jan–1 Feb	Pisces
2 Feb–5 June	Aries
6 June–5 July	Taurus
6 July–1 Aug	Gemini
2–27 Aug	Cancer
28 Aug–21 Sept	Leo
22 Sept–16 Oct	Virgo
17 Oct–9 Nov	Libra
10 Nov–3 Dec	Scorpio
4–26 Dec	Sagittarius
27 Dec–19 Jan 1978	Capricorn

1978

20 Jan–12 Feb	Aquarius
13 Feb–8 Mar	Pisces
9 Mar–1 Apr	Aries
2–26 Apr	Taurus
27 Apr–21 May	Gemini
22 May–15 June	Cancer

16 June–11 July	Leo
12 July–7 Aug	Virgo
8 Aug–6 Sept	Libra
7 Sept–6 Jan 1979	Scorpio

1979

7 Jan–4 Feb	Sagittarius
5 Feb–2 Mar	Capricorn
3–28 Mar	Aquarius
29 Mar–22 Apr	Pisces
23 Apr–17 May	Aries
18 May–10 June	Taurus
11 June–5 July	Gemini
6–29 July	Cancer
30 July–23 Aug	Leo
24 Aug–16 Sept	Virgo
17 Sept–10 Oct	Libra
11 Oct–3 Nov	Scorpio
4–27 Nov	Sagittarius
28 Nov–21 Dec	Capricorn
22 Dec–15 Jan 1980	Aquarius

1980

16 Jan–8 Feb	Pisces
9 Feb–5 Mar	Aries
6 Mar–2 April	Taurus
3 Apr–11 May	Gemini
12 May–4 June	Cancer
5 June–5 Aug	Gemini
6 Aug–6 Sept	Cancer
7 Sept–3 Oct	Leo
4–29 Oct	Virgo
30 Oct–23 Nov	Libra
24 Nov–17 Dec	Scorpio
18 Dec–10 Jan 1981	Sagittarius

1981

11 Jan–3 Feb	Capricorn
4–27 Feb	Aquarius
28 Feb–23 Mar	Pisces
24 Mar–16 Apr	Aries

17 Apr–10 May	Taurus
11 May–4 June	Gemini
5–28 June	Cancer
29 June–23 July	Leo
24 July–17 Aug	Virgo
18 Aug–11 Sept	Libra
12 Sept–8 Oct	Scorpio
9 Oct–4 Nov	Sagittarius
5 Nov–7 Dec	Capricorn
8 Dec–22 Jan 1982	Aquarius

1982

23 Jan–1 Mar	Capricorn
2 Mar–5 Apr	Aquarius
6 Apr–3 May	Pisces
4–29 May	Aries
30 May–24 June	Taurus
25 June–19 July	Gemini
20 July–13 Aug	Cancer
14 Aug–6 Sept	Leo
7 Sept–1 Oct	Virgo
2–25 Oct	Libra
26 Oct–17 Nov	Scorpio
18 Nov–11 Dec	Sagittarius
12 Dec–4 Jan 1983	Capricorn

1983

5–28 Jan	Aquarius
29 Jan–21 Feb	Pisces
22 Feb–18 Mar	Aries
19 Mar–12 Apr	Taurus
13 Apr–8 May	Gemini
9 May–5 June	Cancer
6 June–9 July	Leo
10 July–26 Aug	Virgo
27 Aug–4 Oct	Leo
5 Oct–8 Nov	Virgo
9 Nov–5 Dec	Libra
6–31 Dec	Scorpio

1984

1–24 Jan	Sagittarius
25 Jan–18 Feb	Capricorn
19 Feb–13 Mar	Aquarius
14 Mar–6 Apr	Pisces
7 Apr–1 May	Aries
2–25 May	Taurus
26 May–19 June	Gemini
20 June–13 July	Cancer
14 July–6 Aug	Leo
7–31 Aug	Virgo
1–24 Sept	Libra
25 Sept–19 Oct	Scorpio
20 Oct–12 Nov	Sagittarius
13 Nov–8 Dec	Capricorn
9 Dec–1 Jan 1985	Aquarius

1985

2 Jan–1 Feb	Pisces
2 Feb–5 June	Aries
6 June–5 July	Taurus
6 July–1 Aug	Gemini
2–27 August	Cancer
28 Aug–21 Sept	Leo
22 Sept–15 Oct	Virgo
16 Oct–8 Nov	Libra
9 Nov–2 Dec	Scorpio
3–26 Dec	Sagittarius
27 Dec–19 Jan 1986	Capricorn

1986

20 Jan–12 Feb	Aquarius
13 Feb–8 Mar	Pisces
9 Mar–1 Apr	Aries
2–25 Apr	Taurus
26 Apr–20 May	Gemini
21 May–14 June	Cancer
15 June–10 July	Leo
11 July–6 Aug	Virgo
7 Aug–6 Sept	Libra
7 Sept–6 Jan 1987	Scorpio

1987

7 Jan–4 Feb	Sagittarius
5 Feb–2 Mar	Capricorn
3–27 Mar	Aquarius
28 Mar–21 Apr	Pisces
22 Apr–16 May	Aries
17 May–10 June	Taurus
11 June–4 July	Gemini
5–29 July	Cancer
30 July–22 Aug	Leo
23 Aug–15 Sept	Virgo
16 Sept–9 Oct	Libra
10 Oct–2 Nov	Scorpio
3–27 Nov	Sagittarius
28 Nov–21 Dec	Capricorn
22 Dec–14 Jan 1988	Aquarius

1988

15 Jan–8 Feb	Pisces
9 Feb–5 Mar	Aries
6 Mar–2 Apr	Taurus
3 Apr–16 May	Gemini
17–25 May	Cancer
26 May–5 Aug	Gemini
6 Aug–6 Sept	Cancer
7 Sept–3 Oct	Leo
4–28 Oct	Virgo
29 Oct–22 Nov	Libra
23 Nov–16 Dec	Scorpio
17 Dec–9 Jan 1989	Sagittarius

1989

10 Jan–2 Feb	Capricorn
3–26 Feb	Aquarius
27 Feb–22 Mar	Pisces
23 Mar–15 Apr	Aries
16 Apr–10 May	Taurus
11 May–3 June	Gemini
4–28 June	Cancer
29 June–23 July	Leo
24 July–17 Aug	Virgo

18 Aug–11 Sept	Libra
12 Sept–7 Oct	Scorpio
8 Oct–4 Nov	Sagittarius
5 Nov–9 Dec	Capricorn
10 Dec–15 Jan 1990	Aquarius

1990

16 Jan–2 Mar	Capricorn
3 Mar–5 Apr	Aquarius
6 Apr–3 May	Pisces
4–29 May	Aries
30 May–24 June	Taurus
25 June–19 July	Gemini
20 July–12 Aug	Cancer
13 Aug–6 Sept	Leo
7–30 Sep	Virgo
1–24 Oct	Libra
25 Oct–17 Nov	Scorpio
18 Nov–11 Dec	Sagittarius
12 Dec–4 Jan 1991	Capricorn

1991

5–28 Jan	Aquarius
29 Jan–21 Feb	Pisces
22 Feb–17 Mar	Aries
18 Mar–12 Apr	Taurus
13 Apr–8 May	Gemini
9 May–5 June	Cancer
6 June–10 July	Leo
11 July–20 Aug	Virgo
21 Aug–5 Oct	Leo
6 Oct–8 Nov	Virgo
9 Nov–5 Dec	Libra
6–30 Dec	Scorpio
31 Dec–24 Jan 1992	Sagittarius

1992

25 Jan–17 Feb	Capricorn
18 Feb–12 Mar	Aquarius
13 Mar–6 Apr	Pisces
7–30 Apr	Aries

1–25 May	Taurus
26 May–18 June	Gemini
19 June–12 July	Cancer
13 July–6 Aug	Leo
7–20 Aug	Virgo
21 Aug–24 Sept	Libra
25 Sept–18 Oct	Scorpio
19 Oct–12 Nov	Sagittarius
13 Nov–7 Dec	Capricorn
8 Dec–2 Jan 1993	Aquarius

1993

3 Jan–1 Feb	Pisces
2 Feb–5 June	Aries
6 June–5 July	Taurus
6–31 July	Gemini
1–26 Aug	Cancer
27 Aug–20 Sept	Leo
21 Sep–15 Oct	Virgo
16 Oct–8 Nov	Libra
9 Nov–1 Dec	Scorpio
2–25 Dec	Sagittarius
26 Dec–18 Jan 1994	Capricorn

1994

19 Jan–11 Feb	Aquarius
12 Feb–7 Mar	Pisces
8–31 Mar	Aries
1–25 Apr	Taurus
26 Apr–20 May	Gemini
21 May–14 June	Cancer
15 June–10 July	Leo
11 July–6 Aug	Virgo
7 Aug–6 Sept	Libra
7 Sep–6 Jan 1995	Scorpio

1995

7 Jan–3 Feb	Sagittarius
4 Feb–1 Mar	Capricorn
2–27 Mar	Aquarius
28 Mar–21 Apr	Pisces
22 Apr–15 May	Aries
16 May–9 June	Taurus
10 June–4 July	Gemini
5–28 July	Cancer
29 July–22 Aug	Leo
23 Aug–15 Sept	Virgo
16 Sep–9 Oct	Libra
10 Oct–2 Nov	Scorpio
3–26 Nov	Sagittarius
27 Nov–20 Dec	Capricorn
21 Dec–14 Jan 1996	Aquarius

1996

15 Jan–8 Feb	Pisces
9 Feb–5 Mar	Aries
6 Mar–2 Apr	Taurus
3 Apr–6 Aug	Gemini
7 Aug–6 Sept	Cancer
7 Sept–3 Oct	Leo
4–28 Oct	Virgo
29 Oct–22 Nov	Libra
23 Nov–16 Dec	Scorpio
17 Dec–9 Jan 1997	Sagittarius

1997

10 Jan–2 Feb	Capricorn
3–26 Feb	Aquarius
27 Feb–22 Mar	Pisces
23 Mar–15 Apr	Aries
16 Apr–9 May	Taurus
10 May–3 June	Gemini
4–27 June	Cancer
28 June–22 July	Leo
23 July–16 Aug	Virgo
17 Aug–11 Sept	Libra
12 Sept–7 Oct	Scorpio

8 Oct–4 Nov	Sagittarius
5 Nov–11 Dec	Capricorn
12 Dec–8 Jan 1998	Aquarius

1998

9 Jan–3 Mar	Capricorn
4 Mar–5 Apr	Aquarius
6 Apr–2 May	Pisces
3–28 May	Aries
29 May–23 June	Taurus
24 June–18 July	Gemini
19 July–12 Aug	Cancer
13 Aug–5 Sept	Leo
6–29 Sept	Virgo
30 Sept–23 Oct	Libra
24 Oct–16 Nov	Scorpio
17 Nov–10 Dec	Sagittarius
11 Dec–3 Jan 1999	Capricorn

1999

4–27 Jan	Aquarius
28 Jan–20 Feb	Pisces
21 Feb–17 Mar	Aries
18 Mar–11 Apr	Taurus
12 Apr–7 May	Gemini
8 May–4 June	Cancer
5 June–11 July	Leo
12 July–14 Aug	Virgo
15 Aug–7 Oct	Leo
8 Oct–8 Nov	Virgo
9 Nov–4 Dec	Libra
5–30 Dec	Scorpio
31 Dec–23 Jan 2000	Sagittarius

2000

24 Jan–17 Feb	Capricorn
18 Feb–12 Mar	Aquarius
13 Mar–5 Apr	Pisces
6–30 Apr	Aries
1–14 May	Taurus
15 May–17 June	Gemini

18 June–12 July	Cancer
13 Jul 7–5 Aug	Leo
6–30 Aug	Virgo
31 Aug–23 Sept	Libra
24 Sept–18 Oct	Scorpio
19 Oct–12 Nov	Sagittarius
13 Nov–7 Dec	Capricorn
8 Dec–3 Jan 2001	Aquarius

2001

4 Jan–2 Feb	Pisces
3 Feb–6 June	Aries
7 June–5 July	Taurus
6 July–1 Aug	Gemini
2–26 Aug	Cancer
27 Aug–21 Sept	Leo
22 Sept–15 Oct	Virgo
16 Oct–8 Nov	Libra
9 Nov–2 Dec	Scorpio
3–26 Dec	Sagittarius
27 Dec–19 Jan 2002	Capricorn

2002

20 Jan–12 Feb	Aquarius
13 Feb–8 Mar	Pisces
9 Mar–1 Apr	Aries
2–25 Apr	Taurus
26 Apr–19 May	Gemini
20 May–14 June	Cancer
15 June–10 July	Leo
11 July–7 Aug	Virgo
8 Aug–8 Sept	Libra
9 Sept–7 Jan 2003	Scorpio

2003

8 Jan–4 Feb	Sagittarius
5 Feb–2 Mar	Capricorn
3–27 Mar	Aquarius
28 Mar–21 Apr	Pisces
22 Apr–16 May	Aries
17 May–10 June	Taurus

11 June–4 July	Gemini
5–29 July	Cancer
30 July–22 Aug	Leo
23 Aug–15 Sept	Virgo
16 Sept–9 Oct	Libra
10 Oct–2 Nov	Scorpio
3–27 Nov	Sagittarius
28 Nov–21 Dec	Capricorn
22 Dec–14 Jan 2004	Aquarius

2004

15 Jan–8 Feb	Pisces
9 Feb–5 Mar	Aries
6 Mar–3 Apr	Taurus
4 Apr–7 Aug	Gemini
8 Aug–6 Sept	Cancer
7 Sep–3 Oct	Leo
4–29 Oct	Virgo
30 Oct–22 Nov	Libra
23 Nov–16 Dec	Scorpio
17 Dec–9 Jan 2005	Sagittarius

2005

10 Jan–2 Feb	Capricorn
3–26 Feb	Aquarius
27 Feb–23 Mar	Pisces
24 Mar–15 Apr	Aries
16 Apr–10 May	Taurus
11 May–3 June	Gemini
4–28 June	Cancer
29 June–23 July	Leo
24 July–17 Aug	Virgo
18 Aug–11 Sept	Libra
12 Sept–8 Oct	Scorpio
9 Oct–5 Nov	Sagittarius
6 Nov–15 Dec	Capricorn
16 Dec–1 Jan 2006	Aquarius

2006

2 Jan–5 Mar	Capricorn
6 Mar–6 Apr	Aquarius
7 Apr–2 May	Pisces
3–29 May	Aries
30 May–24 June	Taurus
25 June–19 July	Gemini
20 July–12 Aug	Cancer
13 Aug–6 Sept	Leo
7–30 Sept	Virgo
1–24 Oct	Libra
25 Oct–17 Nov	Scorpio
18 Nov–11 Dec	Sagittarius
12 Dec–3 Jan 2007	Capricorn

2007

4–28 Jan	Aquarius
29 Jan–21 Feb	Pisces
22 Feb–17 Mar	Aries
18 Mar–12 Apr	Taurus
13 Apr–8 May	Gemini
9 May–5 June	Cancer
6 June–14 July	Leo
15 July–9 Aug	Virgo
10 Aug–8 Oct	Leo
9 Oct–8 Nov	Virgo
9 Nov–5 Dec	Libra
6–30 Dec	Scorpio
31 Dec–25 Jan 2008	Sagittarius

2008

26 Jan–17 Feb	Capricorn
18 Feb–13 Mar	Aquarius
14 Mar–6 Apr	Pisces
7–30 Apr	Aries
1–24 May	Taurus
25 May–18 June	Gemini
19 June–12 July	Cancer
13 July–6 Aug	Leo
7–30 Aug	Virgo
31 Aug–25 Sept	Libra

26 Sep–18 Oct	Scorpio
19 Oct–12 Nov	Sagittarius
13 Nov–7 Dec	Capricorn
8 Dec–3 Jan 2009	Aquarius

2009

4 Jan–3 Feb	Pisces
4 Feb–11 Apr	Aries
12–24 Apr	Pisces
25 Apr–6 June	Aries
7 June–5 July	Taurus
6 July–1 Aug	Gemini
2–26 Aug	Cancer
27 Aug–20 Sept	Leo
21 Sep–14 Oct	Virgo
15 Oct–8 Nov	Libra
9 Nov–1 Dec	Scorpio
2–25 Dec	Sagittarius
26 Dec–18 Jan 2010	Capricorn

2010

19 Jan–11 Feb	Aquarius
12 Feb–7 Mar	Pisces
8–31 Mar	Aries
1–25 Apr	Taurus
26 Apr–20 May	Gemini
21 May–14 June	Cancer
15 June–10 July	Leo
11 July–7 Aug	Virgo
8 Aug–8 Sept	Libra
9 Sep–8 Nov	Scorpio
9–31 Nov	Libra
1 Dec–	Scorpio

Astro Quiz

How Venusian Are You?

1 Driving along to meet up with friends, you're ruthlessly cut up by a car full of rowdy kids. Do you manage to resist road rage?

2 A windfall sends you on a shopping spree. You admire a new sports car, but is your choice a set of suede couches for cozy nights in?

3 It's your birthday party. Everyone gasps as an admirer presents you with the latest techno-fabulous cell phone, but do you secretly prefer a bunch of spring flowers brought by the guy in the postroom?

4 After a hard day at work, you daydream of your ideal life: does your fantasy start with designing your dream home décor?

5 An argument has started with an old friend about her new partner. Do you give way to keep the peace and stay buddies?

How Martial Are You?

1 At the crossroads, you're stuck in a line of trucks. You're not in a rush—but can you resist the temptation to rev while the lights are red?

2 Weekends are precious and you really should chill on the couch but would you prefer a trip around town in a new sports car at top speed?

3 After a beer or two you start to daydream about the many goals you want to achieve. Are your first thoughts fantasies of status and power?

4 It's time to work out, so you arrange a tennis game with friends. Although it's not about competition, do you arrive kitted out in the latest gear from top to toe, really needing to win?

5 Working through home chores, you're super-efficient, with programs for every room. Do you need to make progress fast?

The more "yes" answers you score to the Venus questions, the more Venus dominates you. The more "yes" answers you have to the Martial questions, the more Mars holds you in his sway. Look up your Venus and Mars signs (see pages 44 and 62) for further insight.

Venus in the Signs and Houses

Aries or the 1st House

Above all, you value your independence, regardless of who you upset. You love to win, and hate coming second.

Taurus or the 2nd House

When the going gets tough, Taurus goes shopping! You appreciate what you can taste, touch, and feel. You love to laze, but you hate to be poor.

Gemini or the 3rd House

Collecting information and people to amuse and entertain you is your hobby. You love to flirt, but you hate to commit.

Cancer or the 4th House

You value your possessions for their links to the past. You love to nurture, and you hate indifference.

Leo or the 5th House

Bright colors, lavish décor, and fancy restaurants all provide your own personal stage-set. You love to star, and you hate being ignored.

Virgo or the 6th House

You find pleasure in the mundane, value in your work, and see the world in a grain of sand. You love to help, but you hate to be noticed.

Libra or the 7th House

Clashing colors are as upsetting as clashing temperaments. Taste and refinement are as vital as good looks. You love to share, and you hate being alone.

Scorpio or the 8th House

Loyalty and keeping confidences are essential to the financially astute Venus-Scorpio. You love to investigate, but hate to be challenged.

Sagittarius or the 9th House

Flamboyant and sporty, you walk on the wild side, whether it's physical or intellectual. You love to travel, and you hate limitations.

Capricorn or the 10th House

You value your dignity and you'll save that hard-earned cash to get your heart's desire. You love success, but you do hate to look foolish.

Aquarius or the 11th House

You are also fascinated by the unorthodox. You love your freedom, and hate to be tied down.

Pisces or the 12th House

Wandering lonely as a cloud, sometimes only exquisite solitude will satisfy you. You love to unite, and hate cruelty.

6 Understanding Mars

How Do You Get What You Want?

Mars provides your ability to get what you want out of life. Even the most unassuming people need their own Mars qualities to function in life. Your own Mars sign describes how you go about achieving your desires and, while Venus seeks common ground, Mars sometimes delights in difference. Mars in a woman's chart represents her ideal man. For a man, it expresses his power and masculinity. For both men and women, it indicates the nature of their sexual desire. A difficult Mars can mean operating with an imbalance of aggression.

   Like all the planets (with the exception of the Sun and Moon) Mars has periods of retrograde motion, so it can zip through some signs and stay around in others, or dip back into a previous one and then move forward again at various times. Mars is usually no more than a couple of signs from your Sun sign, other than when it is retrograde. Mars is further away from the Sun than the Earth, so its motion is not as fast as that of the Earth. In the table on the following pages, look up your date of birth and read across to discover your Mars sign.

Mars is linked with action—sports, ambition, and the color red

1935

1 Jan–28 Jul	Libra
29 Jul–15 Sep	Scorpio
16 Sept–27 Oct	Sagittarius
28 Oct–6 Dec	Capricorn
7 Dec–13 Jan 1936	Aquarius

1936

14 Jan–21 Feb	Pisces
22–31 Mar	Aries
1 Apr–12 May	Taurus
13 May–24 June	Gemini
25 June–9 Aug	Cancer
10 Aug–25 Sept	Leo
26 Sept–13 Nov	Virgo
14 Nov–4 Jan 1937	Libra

1937

5 Jan–12 Mar	Scorpio
13 Mar–13 May	Sagittarius
14 May–7 Aug	Scorpio
8 Aug–29 Sept	Sagittarius
30 Sept–10 Nov	Capricorn
11 Nov–20 Dec	Aquarius
21 Dec–29 Jan 1938	Pisces

1938

30 Jan–11 Mar	Aries
12 Mar–22 Apr	Taurus
23 Apr–6 June	Gemini
7 June–21 July	Cancer
22 July–6 Sept	Leo
7 Sept–24 Oct	Virgo
25 Oct–10 Dec	Libra
11 Dec–28 Jan 1939	Scorpio

1939

29 Jan–20 Mar	Sagittarius
21 Mar–24 May	Capricorn
25 May–20 July	Aquarius
21 July–23 Sept	Capricorn
24 Sept–18 Nov	Aquarius
19 Nov–4 Jan	Pisces

1940

5 Jan–17 Feb	Aries
18 Feb–1 Apr	Taurus
2 Apr–17 May	Gemini
18 May–3 July	Cancer
4 July–19 Aug	Leo
20 Aug–5 Oct	Virgo
6 Oct–20 Nov	Libra
21 Nov–4 Jan 1941	Scorpio

1941

5 Jan–18 Feb	Sagittarius
19 Feb–2 Apr	Capricorn
3 Apr–16 May	Aquarius
17 May–2 July	Pisces
3 July–11 Jan 1942	Aries

1942

12 Jan–7 Mar	Taurus
8 Mar–25 Apr	Gemini
26 Apr–14 June	Cancer
15 June–1 Aug	Leo
2 Aug–17 Sept	Virgo
18 Sept–1 Nov	Libra
2 Nov–15 Dec	Scorpio
16 Dec–26 Jan 1943	Sagittarius

1943

27 Jan–7 Mar	Capricorn
8 Mar–17 Apr	Aquarius
18 Apr–27 May	Pisces
28 May–7 July	Aries
8 July–23 Aug	Taurus
24 Aug–28 Mar 1944	Gemini

1944

29 Mar–22 May	Cancer
23 May–12 July	Leo
13 July–29 Aug	Virgo
30 Aug–13 Oct	Libra
14 Oct–25 Nov	Scorpio
26 Nov–5 Jan 1945	Sagittarius

1945

6 Jan–14 Feb	Capricorn
15 Feb–25 Mar	Aquarius
26 Mar–2 May	Pisces
3 May–11 June	Aries
12 June–23 July	Taurus
24 July–7 Sept	Gemini
8 Sept–11 Nov	Cancer
12 Nov–26 Dec	Leo
27 Dec–22 Apr 1946	Cancer

1946

23 Apr–20 June	Leo
21 June–9 Aug	Virgo
10 Aug–24 Sept	Libra
25 Sept–6 Nov	Scorpio
7 Nov–17 Dec	Sagittarius
18 Dec–25 Jan	Capricorn

1947

26 Jan–4 Mar	Aquarius
5 Mar–11 Apr	Pisces
12 Apr–21 May	Aries
22 May–1 July	Taurus
2 July–13 Aug	Gemini
14 Aug–1 Oct	Cancer
2 Oct–1 Dec	Leo
2 Dec–12 Feb 1948	Virgo

1948

13 Feb–18 May	Leo
19 May–17 July	Virgo
18 July–8 Sept	Libra
9 Sept–17 Oct	Scorpio
18 Oct–26 Nov	Sagittarius
27 Nov–4 Jan 1949	Capricorn

1949

5 Jan–11 Feb	Aquarius
12 Feb–21 Mar	Pisces
22 Mar–30 Apr	Aries
1 May–10 June	Taurus
11 June–23 July	Gemini
24 July–7 Sept	Cancer
8 Sept–27 Oct	Leo
28 Oct–26 Dec	Virgo
27 Dec–27 Mar 1950	Libra

1950

28 Mar–10 June	Virgo
11 June–9 Aug	Libra
10 Aug–24 Sept	Scorpio
25 Sept–5 Nov	Sagittarius
6 Nov–14 Dec	Capricorn
15 Dec–21 Jan	Aquarius

1951

22 Jan–28 Feb	Pisces
1 Mar–9 Apr	Aries
10 Apr–20 May	Taurus
21 May–2 July	Gemini
3 July–17 Aug	Cancer
18 Aug–4 Oct	Leo
5 Oct–23 Nov	Virgo
24 Nov–19 Jan 1952	Libra

1952

20 Jan–26 Aug	Scorpio
27 Aug–11 Oct	Sagittarius
12 Oct–20 Nov	Capricorn
21 Nov–29 Dec	Aquarius
30 Dec–7 Feb 1953	Pisces

1953

8 Feb–19 Mar	Aries
20 Mar–30 Apr	Taurus
1 May–13 June	Gemini
14 June–28 July	Cancer
29 July–13 Sept	Leo
14 Sept–31 Oct	Virgo
1 Nov–19 Dec	Libra
20 Dec–8 Feb 1954	Scorpio

1954

9 Feb–11 Apr	Sagittarius
12 Apr–2 July	Capricorn
3 July–23 Aug	Sagittarius
24 Aug–20 Oct	Capricorn
21 Oct–3 Dec	Aquarius
4 Dec–14 Jan 1955	Pisces

1955

15 Jan–25 Feb	Aries
26 Feb–9 Apr	Taurus
10 Apr–25 May	Gemini
26 May–10 July	Cancer
11 July–26 Aug	Leo
27 Aug–12 Oct	Virgo
13 Oct–28 Nov	Libra
29 Nov–13 Jan 1956	Scorpio

1956

14 Jan–27 Feb	Sagittarius
28 Feb–13 Apr	Capricorn
14 Apr–2 June	Aquarius
3 June–5 Dec	Pisces
6 Dec–27 Jan 1957	Aries

1957

28 Jan–16 Mar	Taurus
17 Mar–3 May	Gemini
4 May–20 June	Cancer
21 June–7 Aug	Leo
8 Aug–23 Sept	Virgo
24 Sept–7 Nov	Libra
8 Nov–22 Dec	Scorpio
23 Dec–2 Feb 1958	Sagittarius

1958

3 Feb–16 Mar	Capricorn
17 Mar–26 Apr	Aquarius
27 Apr–6 June	Pisces
7 June–20 July	Aries
21 July–20 Sept	Taurus
21 Sept–28 Oct	Gemini
29 Oct–9 Feb 1959	Taurus

1959

10 Feb–9 Apr	Gemini
10 Apr–30 June	Cancer
1–19 July	Leo
20 July–4 Sept	Virgo
5 Sept–20 Oct	Libra
21 Oct–2 Dec	Scorpio
3 Dec–13 Jan 1960	Sagittarius

1960

14 Jan–22 Feb	Capricorn
23 Feb–1 Apr	Aquarius
2 Apr–10 May	Pisces
11 May–19 June	Aries
20 June–1 Aug	Taurus
2 Aug–20 Sept	Gemini
21 Sep–4 Feb 1961	Cancer

1961

5–6 Feb	Gemini
7 Feb–5 May	Cancer
6 May–27 June	Leo
28 June–16 Aug	Virgo
17 Aug–30 Sept	Libra
1 Oct–12 Nov	Scorpio
13 Nov–23 Dec	Sagittarius
24 Dec–31 Jan 1962	Capricorn

1962

1 Feb–11 Mar	Aquarius
12 Mar–18 Apr	Pisces
19 Apr–27 May	Aries
28 May–8 July	Taurus
9 July–21 Aug	Gemini
22 Aug–10 Oct	Cancer
11 Oct–2 June 1963	Leo

1963

3 June–26 July	Virgo
27 July–11 Sept	Libra
12 Sept–24 Oct	Scorpio
25 Oct–4 Dec	Sagittarius
5 Dec–12 Jan 1964	Capricorn

1964

13 Jan–19 Feb	Aquarius
20 Feb–28 Mar	Pisces
29 Mar–6 May	Aries
7 May–16 June	Taurus
17 June–29 July	Gemini
30 July–14 Sept	Cancer
15 Sept–5 Nov	Leo
6 Nov–28 June 1965	Virgo

1965

29 June–19 Aug	Libra
20 Aug–3 Oct	Scorpio
4 Oct–13 Nov	Sagittarius
14 Nov–22 Dec	Capricorn
23 Dec–29 Jan 1966	Aquarius

1966

30 Jan–8 Mar	Pisces
9 Mar–16 Apr	Aries
17 Apr–27 May	Taurus
28 May–10 July	Gemini
11 July–24 Aug	Cancer
25 Aug–11 Oct	Leo
12 Oct–3 Dec	Virgo
4 Dec–11 Feb 1967	Libra

1967

12 Feb–30 Mar	Scorpio
31 Mar–18 July	Libra
19 July–9 Sept	Scorpio
10 Sept–22 Oct	Sagittarius
23 Oct–30 Nov	Capricorn
1 Dec–8 Jan 1968	Aquarius

1968

9 Jan–16 Feb	Pisces
17 Feb–26 Mar	Aries
27 Mar–7 May	Taurus
8 May–20 June	Gemini
21 June–4 Aug	Cancer
5 Aug–20 Sept	Leo

21 Sept–8 Nov	Virgo
9 Nov–28 Dec	Libra
29 Dec–24 Feb 1969	Scorpio

1969

25 Feb–20 Sept	Sagittarius
21 Sept–3 Nov	Capricorn
4 Nov–14 Dec	Aquarius
15 Dec–23 Jan 1970	Pisces

1970

24 Jan–6 Mar	Aries
7 Mar–17 Apr	Taurus
18 Apr–1 June	Gemini
2 June–17 July	Cancer
18 July–2 Sept	Leo
3 Sept–19 Oct	Virgo
20 Oct–5 Dec	Libra
6 Dec–22 Jan 1971	Scorpio

1971

23 Jan–11 Mar	Sagittarius
12 Mar–2 May	Capricorn
3 May–5 Nov	Aquarius
6 Nov–25 Dec	Pisces
26 Dec–9 Feb 1972	Aries

1972

10 Feb–26 Mar	Taurus
27 Mar–11 May	Gemini
12 May–27 June	Cancer
28 June–14 Aug	Leo
15 Aug–29 Sept	Virgo
30 Sept–14 Nov	Libra
15 Nov–29 Dec	Scorpio
30 Dec–11 Feb 1973	Sagittarius

1973

12 Feb–25 Mar	Capricorn
26 Mar–7 May	Aquarius
8 May–19 June	Pisces
20 June–11 Aug	Aries

12 Aug–28 Oct	Taurus
29 Oct–23 Dec	Aries
24 Dec–26 Feb 1974	Taurus

1974

27 Feb–19 Apr	Gemini
20 Apr–8 June	Cancer
9 June–26 July	Leo
27 July–11 Sept	Virgo
12 Sept–27 Oct	Libra
28 Oct–9 Dec	Scorpio
10 Dec–20 Jan 1975	Sagittarius

1975

21 Jan–2 Mar	Capricorn
3 Mar–10 Apr	Aquarius
11 Apr–20 May	Pisces
21 May–30 June	Aries
1 July–13 Aug	Taurus
14 Aug–16 Oct	Gemini
17 Oct–24 Nov	Cancer
25 Nov–17 Mar 1976	Gemini

1976

18 Mar–15 May	Cancer
16 May–5 July	Leo
6 July–23 Aug	Virgo
24 Aug–7 Oct	Libra
8 Oct–19 Nov	Scorpio
20 Nov–31 Dec	Sagittarius

1977

1 Jan–8 Feb	Capricorn
9 Feb–19 Mar	Aquarius
20 Mar–26 Apr	Pisces
27 Apr–5 June	Aries
6 June–16 July	Taurus
17 July–31 Aug	Gemini
1 Sept–25 Oct	Cancer
26 Oct–25 Jan 1978	Leo

1978

26 Jan–9 Apr	Cancer
10 Apr–13 June	Leo
14 June–3 Aug	Virgo
4 Aug–18 Sept	Libra
19 Sept–1 Nov	Scorpio
2 Nov–11 Dec	Sagittarius
12 Dec–19 Jan 1979	Capricorn

1979

20 Jan–26 Feb	Aquarius
27 Feb–6 Apr	Pisces
7 Apr–15 May	Aries
16 May–25 June	Taurus
26 June–7 Aug	Gemini
8 Aug–23 Sept	Cancer
24 Sept–18 Nov	Leo
19 Nov–10 Mar 1980	Virgo

1980

11 Mar–3 May	Leo
4 May–9 July	Virgo
10 July–28 Aug	Libra
29 Aug–11 Oct	Scorpio
12 Oct–21 Nov	Sagittarius
22 Nov–29 Dec	Capricorn
30 Dec–5 Feb 1981	Aquarius

1981

6 Feb–16 Mar	Pisces
17 Mar–24 Apr	Aries
25 Apr–4 June	Taurus
5 June–17 July	Gemini
18 July–1 Sept	Cancer
2 Sept–20 Oct	Leo
21 Oct–15 Dec	Virgo
16 Dec–2 Aug 1982	Libra

1982

3 Aug–19 Sept	Scorpio
20 Sept–30 Oct	Sagittarius
31 Oct–9 Dec	Capricorn
10 Dec–16 Jan 1983	Aquarius

1983

17 Jan–24 Feb	Pisces
25 Feb–4 Apr	Aries
5 Apr–15 May	Taurus
16 May–28 June	Gemini
29 June–12 Aug	Cancer
13 Aug–29 Sept	Leo
30 Sept–17 Nov	Virgo
18 Nov–10 Jan 1984	Libra

1984

11 Jan–16 Aug	Scorpio
17 Aug–4 Oct	Sagittarius
5 Oct–14 Nov	Capricorn
15 Nov–24 Dec	Aquarius
25 Dec–1 Feb 1985	Pisces

1985

2 Feb–14 Mar	Aries
15 Mar–25 Apr	Taurus
26 Apr–8 June	Gemini
9 June–24 July	Cancer
25 July–9 Sept	Leo
10 Sept–26 Oct	Virgo
27 Oct–13 Dec	Libra
14 Dec–1 Feb 1986	Scorpio

1986

2 Feb–27 Mar	Sagittarius
28 Mar–8 Oct	Capricorn
9 Oct–25 Nov	Aquarius
26 Nov–7 Jan 1987	Pisces

1987

8 Jan–19 Feb	Aries
20 Feb–4 Apr	Taurus
5 Apr–20 May	Gemini
21 May–5 July	Cancer
6 July–21 Aug	Leo
22 Aug–7 Oct	Virgo
8 Oct–23 Nov	Libra
24 Nov–7 Jan 1988	Scorpio

1988

8 Jan–21 Feb	Sagittarius
22 Feb–5 Apr	Capricorn
6 Apr–21 May	Aquarius
22 May–12 July	Pisces
13 July–22 Oct	Aries
23–31 Oct	Pisces
1 Nov–18 Jan 1989	Aries

1989

19 Jan–10 Mar	Taurus
11 Mar–28 Apr	Gemini
29 Apr–15 June	Cancer
16 June–2 Aug	Leo
3 Aug–18 Sept	Virgo
19 Sept–3 Nov	Libra
4 Nov–17 Dec	Scorpio
18 Dec–28 Jan 1990	Sagittarius

1990

29 Jan–10 Mar	Capricorn
11 Mar–19 Apr	Aquarius
20 Apr–30 May	Pisces
31 May–11 July	Aries
12 July–30 Aug	Taurus
31 Aug–13 Dec	Gemini
14 Dec–20 Jan 1991	Taurus

1991

21 Jan–2 Apr	Gemini
3 Apr–25 May	Cancer
26 May–14 July	Leo
15 July–31 Aug	Virgo
1 Sep–15 Oct	Libra
16 Oct–28 Nov	Scorpio
29 Nov–8 Jan 1992	Sagittarius

1992

9 Jan–17 Feb	Capricorn
18 Feb–27 Mar	Aquarius
28 Mar–4 May	Pisces
5 May–13 June	Aries
14 June–25 July	Taurus
26 July–11 Sept	Gemini
12 Sept–26 Apr 1993	Cancer

1993

27 Apr–22 June	Leo
23 June–11 Aug	Virgo
12 Aug–26 Sept	Libra
27 Sept–8 Nov	Scorpio
9 Nov–19 Dec	Sagittarius
20 Dec–27 Jan 1994	Capricorn

1994

28 Jan–6 Mar	Aquarius
7 Mar–13 Apr	Pisces
14 Apr–22 May	Aries
23 May–2 July	Taurus
3 July–15 Aug	Gemini
16 Aug–3 Aug	Cancer
4 Oct–11 Dec	Leo
12 Dec–21 Jan 1995	Virgo

1995

22 Jan–24 May	Leo
25 May–20 July	Virgo
21 July–6 Sept	Libra
7 Sept–19 Oct	Scorpio
20 Oct–29 Nov	Sagittarius
30 Nov–7 Jan 1996	Capricorn

1996

8 Jan–14 Feb	Aquarius
15 Feb–23 Mar	Pisces
24 Mar–1 May	Aries
2 May–11 June	Taurus
12 June–24 July	Gemini
25 July–8 Sept	Cancer

9 Sept–29 Oct	Leo
30 Oct–2 Jan 1997	Virgo

1997

3 Jan–7 Mar	Libra
8 Mar–18 June	Virgo
19 June–13 Aug	Libra
14 Aug–27 Sept	Scorpio
28 Sept–8 Nov	Sagittarius
9 Nov–17 Dec	Capricorn
18 Dec–24 Jan 1998	Aquarius

1998

25 Jan–3 Mar	Pisces
4 Mar–12 Apr	Aries
13 Apr–23 May	Taurus
24 May–5 July	Gemini
6 July–19 Aug	Cancer
20 Aug–6 Oct	Leo
7 Oct–26 Nov	Virgo
27 Nov–25 Jan 1999	Libra

1999

26 Jan–4 May	Scorpio
5 May–4 July	Libra
5 July–1 Sept	Scorpio
2 Sept–16 Oct	Sagittarius
17 Oct–25 Nov	Capricorn
26 Nov–3 Jan 2000	Aquarius

2000

4 Jan–11 Feb	Pisces
12 Feb–22 Mar	Aries
23 Mar–2 May	Taurus
3 May–15 June	Gemini
16 June–31 July	Cancer
1 Aug–16 Sept	Leo
17 Sept–3 Nov	Virgo
4 Nov–22 Dec	Libra
23 Dec–14 Feb 2001	Scorpio

2001

15 Feb–8 Sept	Sagittarius
9 Sept–27 Oct	Capricorn
28 Oct–8 Dec	Aquarius
9 Dec–18 Jan 2002	Pisces

2002

19 Jan–1 Mar	Aries
2 Mar–13 Apr	Taurus
14 Apr–28 May	Gemini
29 May–13 June	Cancer
14 July–29 Aug	Leo
30 Aug–14 Oct	Virgo
15 Oct–1 Dec	Libra
2 Dec–17 Jan 2003	Scorpio

2003

18 Jan–4 Mar	Sagittarius
5 Mar–21 Apr	Capricorn
22 Apr–16 June	Aquarius
17 June–16 Dec	Pisces
17 Dec–3 Feb 2004	Aries

2004

4 Feb–21 Mar	Taurus
22 Mar–7 May	Gemini
8 May–22 June	Cancer
23 June–10 Aug	Leo
11 Aug–26 Sept	Virgo
27 Sept–11 Nov	Libra
12 Nov–25 Dec	Scorpio
26 Dec–6 Feb 2005	Sagittarius

2005

7 Feb–20 Mar	Capricorn
21 Mar–1 May	Aquarius
2 May–12 June	Pisces
13 June–28 July	Aries
29 July–17 Feb 2006	Taurus

2006

18 Feb–14 Apr	Gemini
15 Apr–3 June	Cancer
4 June–22 July	Leo
23 July–8 Sept	Virgo
9 Sept–23 Oct	Libra
24 Oct–6 Dec	Scorpio
7 Dec–16 Jan 2007	Sagittarius

2007

17 Jan–26 Feb	Capricorn
27 Feb–6 Apr	Aquarius
7 Apr–15 May	Pisces
16 May–24 June	Aries
25 June–7 Aug	Taurus
8 Aug–28 Sept	Gemini
29 Sept–Dec 31 2008	Cancer

2008

1 Jan–4 Mar	Gemini
5 Mar–9 May	Cancer
10 May–1 July	Leo
2 July–19 Aug	Virgo
20 Aug–4 Oct	Libra
5 Oct–16 Nov	Scorpio
17 Nov–27 Dec	Sagittarius
28 Dec–4 Feb 2009	Capricorn

2009

5 Feb–15 Mar	Aquarius
16 Mar–22 Apr	Pisces
23–31 May	Aries
1 June–12 July	Taurus
13 July–25 Aug	Gemini
26 Aug–16 Oct	Cancer
17 Oct–7 June 2010	Leo

2010

8 June–29 July	Virgo
30 July–14 Sept	Libra
15 Sept–28 Oct	Scorpio
29 Oct–7 Dec	Sagittarius
8 Dec–	Capricorn

Mars in the Signs and Houses

Aries or the 1st House

Courageous and confident, impulsive and enterprising, you prefer to go it alone. You desire independence, and you detest taking orders.

Taurus or the 2nd House

If something is worth doing, you'll see it through right to the end. Your tried-and-tested method is perseverance. You desire quality, and detest being rushed.

Gemini or the 3rd House

Gifted with flashes of brilliance, you have ideas––but someone else needs to do all of the work! You desire variety, and detest routine.

Cancer or the 4th House

You take one step forward and two steps backward, but you always achieve your goals. You desire security, and hate being abandoned.

Leo or the 5th House
Unafraid to take the initiative, your enthusiasm is infectious, but remember to embrace others' ideas. You desire appreciation, and detest being overlooked.

Virgo or the 6th House
You're the maestro of efficiency, but you are your own and everyone else's worst critic. You desire perfection, and detest shoddiness.

Libra or the 7th House
Your diplomacy makes you a great team leader, but manipulation can stir up ill will. You desire partnership, and detest discord.

Scorpio or the 8th House
Unflagging dedication to your objective means you will work till you drop. You desire intensity, but detest interference.

Sagittarius or the 9th House
Enthusiastic at the start, slapdash in the middle, and completely bored by the end—you really need inspiration. You desire significance, and detest pettiness.

Capricorn or the 10th House
You'll move heaven and earth to climb your chosen mountain. You desire authority, but detest triviality.

Aquarius or the 11th House
You may lack the personal touch, but your inventive approach more than makes up for it. You desire a cause, and detest tedium.

Pisces or the 12th House
Imaginative, dreamy, and rarely pushy, you often allow other people to steal your thunder. You desire a vision, and detest mean-spiritedness.

7 Relationships
How Do You Meet Others?

From the formal relationship with your boss or your lawyer to the passion you share with your lover, your relationships are profoundly influenced by astrology, so once again, understanding your birth chart can be the key to harmonizing your relationships and ultimately getting what you want out of life. This chapter shows you how to make the most of your innate love qualities and how to identify and avoid pitfalls.

The positions of the Sun and Moon in your chart show how you experienced your parents when a child. As an adult, the strongest relationships are formed when you are both looking in the same direction rather than gazing at each other. Wildly differing goals (conflicting Suns) or domestic disharmony (antagonistic Moons) can douse even the most passionate flames of love.

The Sun and Moon

Your first relationships were probably with your parents and your Sun and Moon can indicate the type of parenting you received. The Moon represents a mother, and the Sun symbolizes the father. You can see how the Sun and Moon have a bearing on your expectations from adult relationships. For example, if your Moon is in Aries, your mother may have praised your independence, but a Taurus Moon's mom encouraged caution and family values. Gemini Moon's mother was thrilled by each word you learned. Moon in Cancer? The most influential mom—for good or ill! Leo Moon's mother was a drama queen, but courageous. Your mother may have urged you to aim for perfection if your Moon is in Virgo. If your Moon is in Libra, your mom was devoted but shied from confrontation. Scorpio Moon's mother may have frowned on emotional expression. You learned to keep your feelings hidden. Lucky Sagittarius Moon—your mother allowed you the freedom to explore. Capricorn Moon may have learned that mother loved you best when you were well behaved, and Aquarius Moon's mom found it easier when you went to school—babies restricted her freedom. The Moon in Pisces and you may have felt that your mom needed help—you may have even mothered her!

Likewise, your father never let you win just because you were a kid if your Sun is in Aries. If your Sun is in Taurus, daddy probably opened a savings account the day you were born. Having the Sun in Gemini meant your dad was a playmate. Sun in Cancer and your dad probably did more than his fair share of childcare. Leo Sun may have been daddy's precious baby, but Virgo Sun's father taught you to look after yourself. Libra Sun's father loathed rowdy behavior, and Scorpio Sun's dad may have been distant but highly influential. If your Sun is in Sagittarius, your dad encouraged you to be adventurous, but, as a Capricorn Sun, your father praised diligence and ambition. The Sun in Aquarius and daddy may not have been around much—you learned to rely on your peers. Pisces Sun may have had to share his love with a stream of others.

Venus and Mars

Venus and Mars come into their own as you begin the mysterious journey of adult relationships. Compatibility between charts is most easily achieved between planets in sympathetic elements—Fire and Air, or Earth and Water, work well together. However, conflicting elements—Fire and Water, Air and Earth, for example—can ignite the spark of passion and provide the opportunity for personal growth.

When interpreting a chart for a partner or potential mate, the House positions of Venus and Mars can help you to figure out how the object of your affections gets their kicks and where they are busiest. For example, someone with Venus in the 9th House loves to travel, and someone with Mars in the 4th House may be constantly improving the home.

Venus in Love (or How to be Irresistible)

If your Venus sign is...

Aries
Romantic challenges are tantalizing to you, but never forget that the hunter sometimes gets captured—and you may succumb.

Taurus
For Venus Taurus, your love is touchy-feely sensuality. You hold on to love for dear life, as long as you think it's worth it.

Gemini
Once you go off someone, you go off them! Making love can be less exhilarating than making conversation.

Cancer
Dynamite in bed, a wizard in the kitchen—you'll do anything to stave off rejection. But what turns you on? You need attention too.

Leo
Always aiming for the top, you thrive on praise and pampering. You may adore attention, but your loyalty is without question.

Virgo
You're picky about looking neat—yet your calm countenance guards a passionate fire. You are an Earth sign, after all.

Libra
Mr. or Ms. Manners of the zodiac, you love to cosset your lover. However, you are not above gentle manipulation if you feel under threat.

Scorpio
What goes on in the bedroom is just between you and your lover. You need total trust, not casual betrayal.

Sagittarius
Romance is just another game and your naivety is sweet. You hate to be tied down, but your frankness shocks the more bashful lover.

Capricorn
Your status is important and you are put off by public affection. However, you love a touch of undercover naughtiness.

Aquarius
A liberated attitude means friends are as important as lovers. Your space-versus-intimacy dilemma confuses some.

Pisces
Venus exalted, you feel universal, unbounded love—lame ducks apply here. However, the clandestine affair is your forte.

Mars in the Bedroom (and How to Stay There)

If your Mars sign is...

Aries
Initial passion quickly wears off—you prefer them hard to get. You love to have your head rubbed. Develop patience.

Taurus
Breakfast in bed, anyone? You have sensuality in spades. You love having your neck kissed. Develop detachment.

Gemini
Mental stimulation gets your juices flowing—boredom sends you packing. You love to have your fingers sucked. Develop warmth.

Cancer
Moods affect your desire and imaginative foreplay is a must. You love to have your stomach massaged. Develop directness.

Leo
You put on a performance par excellence. Appreciation increases desire—ridicule crushes it. You love to have your mane stroked. Develop generosity.

Virgo
Clean teeth and crisp sheets are a must. Encouragement opens up your latent sensuality. You love back massages. Develop spontaneity.

Libra

Soft lights, music, and ambient perfume in the air are essential to enhance your mood. You love the gentle stroking of your lower back. Develop sharing.

Scorpio

Anyone afraid of intimacy should approach with caution. You love the sensation of all-over touch. Develop objectivity.

Sagittarius

The more the merrier—goodwill and a giggle out-rank fidelity and technique. You love to have your thighs caressed. Develop sensitivity.

Capricorn

Dressing up and role-play takes your mind off your work and onto your lover. You love to have your bone structure admired. Develop tranquility.

Aquarius

You approach love-making as though it were an experiment. You love to have your ankles fondled. Develop intimacy.

Pisces

The "little death" is as good a route as any in your quest for wholeness. You love to have your toes kissed. Develop emotional armor.

Passionate and Platonic: Venus and Mars

We fall in love for many different reasons—but sometimes, the most thrilling relationships quickly burn out, and long-term partnerships slide from passionate to platonic in the blink of an eye. You can see why, if you compare your Venus and Mars with those of current and previous partners. You can also figure out how to keep the fire of love roaring next time you find yourself falling (see the sections on Venus and Mars in the bedroom on pages 78–81). Look at the lists below. For example, if your Venus or Mars sign is Aries and your partner's Venus or Mars sign is Sagittarius (or the other way around) you should share passion— but an Aries and Cancer partnership may end up decidedly chilly.

Hot romance
(Venus and Mars,
Mars and Venus)

Aries and Sagittarius
Taurus and Capricorn
Gemini and Aquarius
Cancer and Capricorn
Leo and Libra
Virgo and Pisces
Libra and Leo
Scorpio and Scorpio
Sagittarius and Aries
Capricorn and Taurus
Aquarius and Gemini
Pisces and Cancer

Cold company
(Venus and Mars,
Mars and Venus)

Aries and Cancer
Taurus and Aries
Gemini and Taurus
Cancer and Aquarius
Leo and Aquarius
Virgo and Sagittarius
Libra and Scorpio
Scorpio and Aquarius
Sagittarius and Taurus
Capricorn and Gemini
Aquarius and Cancer
Pisces and Aquarius

Friends and Foes: Mars, Venus, and the Moon

What about all the other relationships that are important in your life? Who's your best friend? Who did you enjoy rooming with, and who nearly drove you insane? Remember, if you really want to, you can get along with anyone—but you may have to learn to think like them. To find out about best friends, use your Moon and Venus signs. As with the love combinations (see opposite) check out any Moon Venus combination: For example, if your Moon sign is Sagittarius and a new friend's Venus sign is Aries, it's likely that you'll become firm friends. To check out your potential enemies, use your Mars signs only.

Best friends
(Moon and Venus,
Venus and Moon)

Aries and Sagittarius
Taurus and Capricorn
Gemini and Virgo
Cancer and Pisces
Leo and Libra
Virgo and Gemini
Libra and Leo
Scorpio and Cancer
Sagittarius and Aquarius
Capricorn and Scorpio
Aquarius and Aries
Pisces and Taurus

Worst enemies
(Mars and Mars)

Aries and Scorpio
Taurus and Leo
Gemini and Scorpio
Cancer and Aries
Leo and Scorpio
Virgo and Sagittarius
Libra and Cancer
Capricorn and Aquarius
Pisces and Sagittarius

Domestic Bliss and Domestic Chaos: The Moon

The Moon is the key to domestic bliss or chaos, because of its association with the home and intimacy. Check out the Moon sign combinations below to see who are your ideal housemates (or partners you live with) and who to avoid at all costs.

House of harmony
(Moon and Moon)

Aries and Sagittarius
Taurus, Virgo, and Capricorn
Gemini and Aquarius
Leo and Libra
Scorpio and Virgo
Aquarius, Gemini, and Sagittarius
Pisces, Cancer, and Scorpio

House of horror
(Moon and Moon)

Aries and Scorpio
Taurus and Gemini
Cancer and Aquarius
Leo and Capricorn
Virgo and Sagittarius
Libra and Pisces
Scorpio and Sagittarius

Office Allies and Adversaries: Mars and the Sun

The Sun and Mars together represent action, the outward aspects of your personality that you show to others. At work, who can you rely upon—and who can't be trusted? Use your Sun and Mars signs to discover who can help or who can hinder you.

Allies
(Sun and Mars, Mars and Sun)

Aries and Leo
Taurus and Scorpio
Gemini and Libra
Cancer and Virgo
Leo and Sagittarius
Virgo and Scorpio
Libra and Aquarius
Scorpio and Capricorn
Sagittarius and Gemini
Capricorn and Virgo
Aquarius and Sagittarius
Pisces and Virgo

Adversaries
(Sun and Mars, Mars and Sun)

Aries and Taurus
Taurus and Sagittarius
Gemini and Scorpio
Cancer and Aries
Leo and Aquarius
Virgo and Gemini
Libra and Aries
Scorpio and Pisces
Sagittarius and Virgo
Capricorn and Gemini
Aquarius and Taurus
Pisces and Aries

Comparing Your Charts

A little friction often serves to stimulate attraction between lovers, but there must be some sympathy between your birth charts for any relationship to have long-term potential. You are now going to be introduced to the astrological secrets that explain whether your existing or future relationship is one of enduring love, or just a fleeting, uncommitted affair. This is where you learn the true importance of your Rising sign as well as the Sun, Moon, Venus, and Mars signs. You can also discover how the elemental balance can enhance or mar a relationship with someone who initially makes you go weak at the knees.

The Link Between Rising Signs

One vital love link between two charts is planets from one chart connected to the Rising sign, or Ascendant, of the other. For example, if you have Gemini Rising, its opposite sign Sagittarius will be on the cusp of the 7th House of committed relationships. Someone with the Sun, Moon, Venus or Mars in Gemini or Sagittarius will be attracted to you and vice versa. The more planets in these signs, the more potential! If the charts have Ascendants in the same or opposing signs, then compatibility skyrockets. But these are only one of the clues in this romantic treasure hunt.

Let's look at interplanetary connections. This is when the elements begin to make their presence felt. The Earth and Water elements harmonize, as do Air and Fire. This harmony is also expressed as a good aspect on the Astro wheel. So Fiery Aries is sextile (two signs away from) Airy Gemini and trine (four signs away from) Fiery Leo. Fire/Air and Fire/Fire are therefore harmonious element pairings. Three signs away, or square, is Watery Cancer. A square aspect is a difficult, or challenging, aspect in astrology, which reflects the elemental incompatibility of Fire and Water—two energies that extinguish each other. Try using your sign to start familiarizing yourself with the elements and aspects.

Suns and Moons

The Sun is vital in relationships, and compatibility is usually found when your lover's Sun is trine or sextile your own. Because your approach to life is similar, you have a compatible but not identical outlook. Suns in the same or opposite sign can go either way—mutual understanding or permanent loggerheads! If there are enough other indications of mutual compatibility, it could just work. Suns three signs apart often feel irritated by each other.

Harmony between the Sun and Moon can indicate that a relationship will prosper and develop. The Sun and Moon next to each other is a fabulous combination. This is even better if it happens both ways around—with your Sun next to his Moon and his Sun next to your Moon. But any positive links between the Sun and Moon boost the chances of a marathon rather than a sprint.

There will be sympathy between you if Venus in one chart is either in the same sign, or linked positively to the Sun, Moon, or Mars in the other chart. If Mars is harmonizing with the Sun or Moon, you will energize and excite each other. However, Mars opposite or in the same sign as the Sun could lead to major clashes. Mars in the same combination with the Moon may mean that one partner dominates.

An incredibly sexy combination is Venus in the same sign, sextile, or trine, Mars—your Venus in Leo and their Mars in Libra, Sagittarius, Gemini or Aries, say. Opposites do initially attract, but Venus opposite or three signs away from Mars may promise mutual fireworks but only manage to deliver damp squibs!

Using the Astro Wheel for Compatibility

How do you know if your partner is just a fling or the one? Find the Astro wheel on pages 16–19 that has your Rising sign aligned with the first House. On pages 94–143, find the profiles for Mr. or Ms. Gorgeous' Sun, Moon, Venus, and Mars signs. Mark their positions around the wheel along with your own Sun, Moon, Venus, and Mars. You can see how their planets link up with your own and into which Houses they fall. If any of their planets (except Mars) fall into your 7th and 4th House, it can indicate understanding from the first meeting. If you have their birth time and Rising sign, you can find insight on how he or she experiences you—simply repeat the process, this time find the Astro wheel on pages 16–19 with their Rising sign aligned with the first House, marking their Sun, Moon, Venus, and Mars around the wheel followed by your own. Note down the relationships between both sets of planets, not forgetting links to the Ascendant and its opposite sign. Turn to the unique scoring system overleaf to discover if this is true love.

Sextile means two signs apart.

Trine means four signs apart.

Square means three signs apart.

Opposite means six signs apart; opposite one another on the zodiac wheel.

- (minus) 7–10 points - Quit now, or keep it very casual.

11–15 points - Needs work, but may be worth it.

16–20 points - Hot, but not boiling.

21–30 points - Jackpot!

Compatibility Questionnaire

Ascendants, or Rising sign, opposite or in the same sign	3
Sun, Moon, Venus, Mars opposite or next to Rising sign	3
Sun trine or sextile Sun	2
Sun in same or opposite sign as Sun	1
Sun square Sun	1
Sun in same sign as Moon	3
Sun trine or sextile Moon	2
Sun opposite or square Moon	1
Sun, Moon, or Venus in the 4th House	3
Sun sextile or trine Venus	2
Sun opposite or square Venus	1
Moon opposite Moon	1
Moon square Moon	-1
Moon in same sign, sextile, or trine Moon	2
Moon sextile or trine Venus	2
Moon opposite, sextile, or trine Venus	2
Moons square Venus	-1
Venus next to, sextile or trine Venus	1
Venus sextile or trine Ascendant	1
Venus square or opposite Venus	1
Venus next to, sextile or trine Mars	3
Venus opposite Mars	1
Venus square Mars	-1
Mars next to, sextile or trine Sun or Moon	1
Mars opposite, trine, or sextile Ascendant	1
Mars next to Ascendant	-1
Mars opposite or square Sun or Moon	-2
Mars in 4th or 7th House	-1
Mars in same or opposite sign Mars	-2

8 Transits

When is the Best Time to Act?

Hindsight is a wonderful thing, but wouldn't you love to have an idea of what was just around the corner? By using this book to plan ahead, you will be able to judge the general mood and also identify the best time to take action. As the planets "transit" through the heavens from one sign to the next, they continue to exert an influence on your chart.

To create a prediction, choose a date in the future than you want a prediction for—this may be an important anniversary such as a birthday or New Year. Next, look up the Sun, Moon, Mars, and Venus signs for that date—on the website www.astrotheme.com, you can find out which signs the planets will be in on a particular date in the future. Just as you did for your birth chart, mark the positions of the planets' signs around the outside of the Astro wheel on pages 16–19 that has your Rising sign aligned with the 1st House. Read the predictions for the planets in the signs and Houses on pages 94–143. For example, if you have the Moon in Cancer in your 9th House, look up Moon in Cancer (the 4th House) and Moon in Sagittarius (the 9th House) for extra insight.

The Sun and Moon in Transit

The Sun in transit

The Sun's journey through each sign takes a year. When he is back at base in your chart he has "returned." That is the origin of the greeting "Many Happy Returns"— your birthday is your Solar Return. The Solar Return is an opportunity to make a fresh start—your own personal "New Year". The Sun moving through your Houses encourages you to make decisions and initiate necessary changes in each area of your life.

Moon in the 4th, 8th, or 12th House: time to withdraw

Moon in 2nd, 3rd, or 6th House: time for self-improvement

Moon in the 1st, 5th, 7th, or 11th House: time to socialize

Moon in the 9th, or 10th House: time for ambition and goals

New Moon: new beginnings

Full Moon: endings

The Moon in transit

The Moon moves through all the signs in just a month—the word "month" is derived from "moon." Her influence is the easiest to connect with, because of her association with moods and feelings. If the Moon is in one of your sensitive and introverted Houses, such as the 4th, 8th, or 12th, you may need to withdraw a little. If she is dancing through your 1st or 7th, you crave attention and company.

When the Moon is new, she is next to the Sun, providing a huge concentration of energy. A New Moon in a House indicates the start of something connected with that House. In the 10th, it ushers in a new phase in your career or even a new job. In the 3rd, a new neighbor could influence your life. The Full Moon around two weeks later may coincide

with endings, as the Moon is opposite the Sun and the atmosphere is volatile. For the two-and-a-half days during which the Moon is in each sign, the emotional environment takes on the quality of that sign. For example, the Moon in Cancer makes for an over-sensitive atmosphere, whereas Sagittarius Moons encourage reckless behavior. A Moon diary is a good way to track her influence on your life.

Venus in Transit

Venus usually spends just under a month in one sign. Occasionally, she appears to stand still, move backwards, then change direction, so you may have to go over old ground. A previous lover may reappear or your current relationship might reach a crisis. When Venus backtracks, or is in "retrograde," you will have another bite of that cherry you thought

had passed you by! Do you have Venus in your 6th House? Look for love at work. Moving through your 9th House, a holiday romance is possible. Whatever House she is transiting, you'll find that your approach to that House's issues becomes more creative and friendly.

Mars in Transit

Mars normally occupies a sign for just over a month and also has periods of retrograde motion when you may find frustration building. Mars urges you to take action in whatever House it is passing through. To get the best from Mars, think of the sign as well as the House. In Virgo, there's obsession with detail and in Taurus, relaxation. Conflict is possible

when Mars transits any of your Houses. Your urge to act for your own best interests will be challenged by others if you forget to consider their feelings. You'll usually feel the need to take action on at least one issue represented by the House Mars is transiting. Mars and Venus together represent the magic of love. When the Sun, Venus, and Mars fall in one sign, look to the nature of the House. So if the planets fall in your 6th House, or career, it's likely that you'll discover love at work. If a New Moon falls there at the same time, enjoy the new beginnings she brings.

Key to the Zodiac Symbols

  Aries
*March 21–
April 20*

  Libra
*September 24–
October 23*

  Taurus
*April 21–
May 21*

 Scorpio
*October 24–
November 22*

  Gemini
*May 22–
June 21*

 Sagittarius
*November 23–
December 21*

 Cancer
*June 22–
July 23*

  Capricorn
*December 22–
January 20*

  Leo
*July 24–
August 23*

  Aquarius
*January 21–
February 19*

  Virgo
*August 24–
September 23*

  Pisces
*February 20–
March 20*

The Planets
in the Signs
and Houses

Sun in Aries
or the 1st House
March 21–April 20

Aims to be:
Ambitious • Decisive • A leader
Adventurous • Optimistic

Sometimes:
Bossy • Tactless • Argumentative
Combative • Domineering

In transit through Aries or the 1st House
Consider this an alternative New Year's Day!
Now is the perfect time to read self-
improvement manuals and put ideas into
practice. Working and acting alone comes
easiest now, so you may have to put joint
projects on hold. Spring-cleaning and list-
making will occupy your time. While it's right
to concentrate on your own needs, try not to
neglect those closest to you.

Moon in Aries
or the 1st House

Feelings are:
Open • Responsible • Straightforward
Protective • Immediate

Occasionally:
Sulky • Insensitive • Thoughtless
Impatient • Self-centered

In transit through Aries or the 1st House
Your emotions are on the surface and you may
be looking for some extra attention from those
close to you. The downside is that you may
appear emotionally demanding. However, you
have sympathy to spare and you are willing to
listen to anyone in need. You are supersensitive
now, so be sure that what you feel is really
coming from you rather than what you've
absorbed from those around you.

Venus in Aries or the 1st House

Values:
Courage • Passion • Honesty
Independence • Generosity

Occasionally:
Overbearing • Rude • Competitive
Hasty • Impulsive

In transit through Aries or the 1st House
This is not the time to hide away at home,
as you will be in demand from family, friends,
colleagues, and potential lovers. If you are
looking for someone special to share your
dreams, this is the time to revamp your social
life. You may also be asked to soothe conflict,
as you are filled with the spirit of compromise.
Getting your own way seems less important
than peace, love and understanding.

Mars in Aries
or the 1st House

Usually:
Spontaneous • Pioneering • Enterprising
Independent • Assertive

Sometimes:
Rash • Impulsive • Ruthless • Egotistical
Aggressive

In transit through Aries or the 1st House
It's best to maintain your independence now as
cooperation may cramp your style. Impressing
the boss is easy, but friends and family may find
you a touch insensitive; you may be set on
furthering your own interests, but try not to step
on too many toes in the process. If you are
predominantly Fire or Air you will feel ready to
take on the world. If your chart is mainly Water
or Earth, balance activity with enough rest.

Sun in Taurus
or the 2nd House

April 21–May 21

Aims to be:
Tolerant • Kindly • Consistent
Steady • Productive

Sometimes:
Self-indulgent • Obstinate • Smug
Dogged • Stolid

In transit through Taurus or the 2nd House
Consolidating your assets is a wise move
when Taurus is under the spotlight. Money
and possessions are only part of the picture;
resist the urge to identify yourself solely in
relation to what you own. Remember, you are
your main resource and best asset. Updating
your resumé, devising new strategies, or
checking out educational classes are all
positive uses of Taurean energy.

Moon in Taurus or the 2nd House

Feelings are:
Stable • Enduring • Loyal
Serene • Nurturing

Occasionally:
Greedy • Dogmatic • Jealous
Sentimental • Envious

In transit through Taurus or the 2nd House
Indulging in major retail therapy may seem
the obvious thing to do during this transit.
However, as with so many of life's temptations,
you'll most likely regret it later. Wait for a few
days before you spend your hard-earned cash.
It would be far better to organize a get-together
with friends or family, directing all that sensual
energy into preparing a sumptuous and
heart-warming meal.

Venus in Taurus or the 2nd House

Values:
Affection • Beauty • Luxury
Sensuality • Nature

Occasionally:
Possessive • Acquisitive • Covetous
Jealous • Decadent

In transit through Taurus or the 2nd House
Venus is at home here and you may find that
a financial opportunity or a windfall comes your
way. If you need to borrow some money, this
is a good time to approach your bank manager.
Investments get a real boost and if you have
been thinking of a big purchase, such as a
new home or car, now you can put your plans
into action. Sensuality is emphasized and this
will influence many areas of your life. Enjoy!

Mars in Taurus
or the 2nd House

Usually:
Constructive • Composed • Strong-willed
Patient • Reliable

Sometimes:
Inflexible • Stubborn • Slow
Insistent • Uncompromising

In transit through Taurus or the 2nd House
Actively seeking to improve your financial
situation is one thing, but you are not your bank
account: possessions can enhance your life,
but they don't define it. The bargain you just
had to have may be another white elephant,
especially if your chart is biased toward Fire
or Air. Watery types may be looking for emotional
reassurance from partners and family. If your
chart is mainly Earth, you are more likely to
make positive investments.

Sun in Gemini or the 3rd House

May 22–June 21

Aims to be:
Witty • Friendly • Enquiring
Accommodating • Cheerful

Sometimes:
Ambiguous • Amoral • Unreliable
Unstable

In transit through Gemini or the 3rd House
Communication is key now. If you've been avoiding a tricky discussion, especially with someone you come into daily contact with, broach the subject now. But communication is a two-way street—listen as well as talk. While your social life may be very busy, you may find that you are bursting with ideas. Noting your thoughts in a diary could help you separate reality from fantasy.

Moon in Gemini or the 3rd House

Feelings are:
Light • Diverse • Multifaceted
Restless • Playful

Occasionally:
Insincere • Superficial • Inconsistent
Shallow • Fickle

In transit through Gemini or the 3rd House
Objectivity may have taken a short break for a couple of days as it seems that you and everyone else is determined to get what's bugging them out in the open once and for all. If you can stop talking just long enough to reflect for a moment, you may realize that reality is completely obscured by an inability to see anyone else's viewpoint. Definitely a time to keep your thoughts to yourself rather than telling it like it is!

Venus in Gemini or the 3rd House

Values:
Eloquence • Curiosity • Intelligence
Versatility • Communication

Occasionally:
Deceptive • Unsympathetic • Slippery
Capricious • Artful

In transit through Gemini or the 3rd House
Socializing locally suddenly seems a much more intriguing prospect, and you may discover that your neighborhood has far more to offer than you thought. Any contact with your siblings takes on an affectionate note and, if there are any disagreements that need to be resolved, now's the time to make up. Make sure you never leave the house looking anything but your best, as love may appear in the most mundane circumstances.

Mars in Gemini or the 3rd House

Usually:
Lively • Alert • Enthusiastic
Inquisitive • Talkative

Sometimes:
Glib • Cutting • Nosy
Insubstantial • Trivial

In transit through Gemini or the 3rd House
During this energetic transit you will be very busy—which is fantastic if you have a specific project to work on, and even better if it can involve neighbors or siblings. But if you are at a loose end, interfering with other people's business without an invitation could evoke a less than neighborly response. If you really are looking for something to do, you could volunteer your services for a local project.

Sun in Cancer or the 4th House

June 22–July 23

Aims to be:
Kind • Understanding • Sympathetic
Sensitive • Caring

Sometimes:
Clannish • Picky • Reserved
Over-anxious • Fearful

In transit through Cancer or the 4th House
The closer you stick to people, places, and activities that make you feel secure, the happier you will be—so this is not the best time to make sweeping changes. Take a moment to stop and reflect and you'll be amazed at the inspiration and insight you gain. You are extra-sensitive at the moment, so don't take careless remarks from loved ones to heart.

Moon in Cancer
or the 4th House

Feelings are:
Nourishing • Containing • Receptive
Motherly (either sex) • Shy

Occasionally:
Over-sensitive • Moody • Touchy
Self-pitying • Apprehensive

In transit through Cancer or the 4th House

Home is where the heart is, and you may not
want to stray too far from familiar surroundings
and faces. Occasionally this position can bring
on a fit of the blues and you may resort to
comfort eating or negative attention-grabbing
techniques. Instead, spend as much time as
possible close to water—scented baths provide
that womb-like sensation that we all crave after
a bout of grappling with the outside world.

Venus in Cancer or the 4th House

Values:
Home life • Family • Feelings
Thrift • Security

Occasionally:
Mean • Sentimental • Devious
Clingy • Grasping

In transit through Cancer or the 4th House

You might find it hard to prise yourself away from your own home. Not only do you prefer the company of your family or partner, but the outside world seems a little bit overwhelming. Even the most career-minded may suddenly discover a keen interest in interior décor and whether you are up for a complete makeover or just a few minor touches, your personal living space is likely to be more beautiful at the end of this transit.

Mars in Cancer
or the 4th House

Usually:
Protective • Tenacious • Shrewd
Cautious • Conservative

Sometimes:
Defensive • Tearful • Backward-looking
Irascible • Sullen

In transit through Cancer or the 4th House
You may lose your temper for no apparent
reason at the moment. Of course there is a
reason—but you may have to dig deep to find it.
Mars here stirs up feelings that you may have
pushed aside and, if you have felt used and
abused over the last year, someone blameless
may get the brunt of your anger. Before you
attack others, first take a good look at yourself
and face up to anything you don't much like.

Sun in Leo or the 5th House

July 24–August 23

Aims to be:
Dignified • Creative • Magnanimous
Idealistic • Benevolent

Sometimes:
Condescending • Patronizing • Opinionated
Bossy • Pompous

In transit through Leo or the 5th House
Your adorable inner child is bursting to come
out to play, and pleasure and self-expression
are what you should be concentrating on.
You may also find that while you are enjoying
yourself, you are surprisingly attractive to others.
This is not the time to hide away, so accept
every invitation and perfect your flirtation
techniques. Once-in-a-lifetime experiences
are a possibility now.

Moon in Leo
or the 5th House

Feelings are:
Loyal • Joyful • Optimistic • Loving • Generous

Occasionally:
Demanding • Conceited • Egotistical
Arrogant • Pretentious

In transit through Leo or the 5th House
You are unlikely to keep quiet about your feelings
during this transit. You might not usually be
known as a drama queen, but you could win
an Oscar right now. Rather than throw a tantrum,
immerse yourself in whatever makes you feel
good—whether it's a weepy video or a workout
at the gym. Your protective instincts are well to
the fore and any activity involving children will
give you great pleasure.

Venus in Leo or the 5th House

Values:
Self-expression • Fidelity • Sincerity
Drama • Appreciation

Occasionally:
Predatory • Exhibitionist • Attention-seeking
Imperious • Vain

In transit through Leo or the 5th House
Venus in Leo heralds fun, and it is likely that
you will now be at your most alluring; maybe
it's because you know you have permission
to indulge in anything, as long as it gives you
pure pleasure. If you are seeking a light-hearted
affair, it's likely to present itself during this
transit. Little can thwart your charisma;
arguments will be short-lived, and you
will enjoy the general atmosphere of
goodwill around you.

Mars in Leo
or the 5th House

Usually:
Magnetic • Confident • Straightforward
Proud • Glamorous

Occasionally:
Wilful • Outspoken • Overdressed
Autocratic • Flashy

In transit through Leo or the 5th House
Anyone who dares to cramp your style during
this transit should think twice. You unconsciously
ooze smoldering sensuality—and your impact
on those around you is certainly something to
behold. Asserting yourself comes so naturally
and, what's more, completely devoid of any
unnecessary aggression. Know that you can
get it if you really want it—so make up your
mind and make your move!

Sun in Virgo or the 6th House

August 24–September 23

Aims to be:
Conscientious • Organized • Prudent
Perfectionist • Industrious

Sometimes:
Over-critical • Pedantic • Unimaginative
Tetchy • Puritanical

In transit through Virgo or the 6th House
Your routines come under intense scrutiny and unfortunately it may seem that your needs are also taking second place to everyone else's. The reality is that you could be making much better use of your time and energy, giving yourself far less stress. Consider exactly how you organize your regular chores; you may discover that some of your activities are way past their use-by date.

Moon in Virgo or the 6th House

Feelings are:
Concerned • Self-effacing • Modest
Controlled • Unobtrusive

Occasionally:
Distant • Cold • Intolerant
Dispassionate • Worrisome

In transit through Virgo or the 6th House
Resist the temptation to give yourself a hard time
for any uncharacteristic emotional outbursts over
the last few days—it probably cleared the air. You
need to allow yourself some good old-fashioned
pampering now. Delicious, healthy food,
a couple of early nights and you'll be back
to normal. If you're a pet owner, you won't
need reminding what good listeners they are—
so tell them all about your bad behavior.

Venus in Virgo
or the 6th House

Values:
Discrimination • Adaptability • Good grooming
Dedication • Consideration

Occasionally:
Hesitant • Fussy • Unresponsive
Clinical • Exacting

In transit through Virgo or the 6th House
While fun and games may suddenly come
to an abrupt halt and you have to turn your
attention to more mundane matters, this is
a great time to improve relationships with
work colleagues. You may find that someone
you see every day suddenly appears much
more attractive. The urge for self-improvement
may overwhelm even the most self-indulgent,
and you could find yourself fighting for a space
at the gym or pool.

Mars in Virgo
or the 6th House

Usually:
Practical • Methodical • Efficient
Hardworking • Meticulous

Occasionally:
Workaholic • Servile • Plodding
Complaining • Calculating

In transit through Virgo or the 6th House
It's time to put your house in order—at home
and at work, you zip through your chores like
a whirlwind. While it is usually advisable to
keep in mind the bigger picture, now it's okay
to concentrate on the details. Even the most
self-effacing will find it difficult to take orders
from others, so work alone if possible. Don't
bottle up irritation—speaking your mind
prevents epic-scale resentment.

Sun in Libra or the 7th House

September 24–October 23

Aims to be:
Agreeable • Sociable • Peaceable
Cooperative • Diplomatic

Sometimes:
Interfering • Superficial • Backsliding
Indecisive • Ingratiating

In transit through Libra or the 7th House
You now focus on your most important partnerships and learn a lot about yourself from your relationships with others; the closer they are, the more important the lessons. Too much flexibility can be as damaging as stubbornness in both personal and professional relationships. Use the Sun's positive energy to heal any rifts. Stalled partnership projects will now get fresh impetus.

Moon in Libra
or the 7th House

Feelings are:
Tender • Kind • Affectionate
Romantic • Understanding

Occasionally:
Evasive • Unreliable • Placatory
Hedonistic • Bland

In transit through Libra or the 7th House
The old saying "What you send out returns to you" is never truer than when the Moon is here. Dealings with others are far more emotional than usual and sometimes a personal score may get settled. If someone is provoking you, try to think about what it is that is getting under your skin. You may find that what irritates you most are your own less positive characteristics, just reflected back at you through another person.

Venus in Libra or the 7th House

Values:
Good manners • Partnerships • Good taste
Sharing • Courtesy

Occasionally:
Procrastinating • Ambivalent • Detached
Gullible • Lukewarm

In transit through Libra or the 7th House
Partnerships of all kinds are enhanced as there seems to be much more willingness on everyone's part to put any differences to one side. It's much more pleasurable to share your time with your closest friends or someone extra-special, than going it alone. You may find it much easier to express your feelings, and even the most difficult relationship will benefit. If you are feeling lonely, it's time to shine and attract that soul mate.

Mars in Libra
or the 7th House

Usually:
Impartial • Balanced • Fair • Compromising
Tranquil

Sometimes:
Intolerant • Competitive • Argumentative
Over-dependent • Contentious

In transit through Libra or the 7th House
Mars can be uncomfortable in this position;
Libra and the 7th are all about cooperation,
whereas Mars is ego unbound. Conflict can
arise in the most innocuous situations now, but
it may serve a useful purpose: if you've been too
eager to compromise and feel taken for granted,
you could now have the confidence to stand
up for yourself. Those who don't take you
seriously need reminding that it's time they
changed their minds.

Sun in Scorpio or the 8th house

October 24–November 22

Aims to be:
Purposeful • Strong-willed • Thorough
Profound • Steadfast

Sometimes:
Critical • Ruthless • Spiteful
Unforgiving • Repressed

In transit through Scorpio or the 8th House
Hidden and surface issues are equally
important. Your intuition is keen, but this
sensitivity may create an occasional
misunderstanding. If you are concerned
about someone's behavior, think before you
act. A wiser way to spend your time is figuring
out how to restructure or repay any outstanding
debts. Partnerships that are financial as well
as emotional may need some attention.

Moon in Scorpio or the 8th House

Feelings are:
Perceptive • Deep • Self-protective
Steadfast • Enigmatic

Occasionally:
Obsessive • Devious • Suspicious
Morbid • Vengeful

In transit through Scorpio or the 8th House
Remember to take a reality check every so often
during this transit. Your feelings are super-intense
and you could start believing in off-the-wall
conspiracy theories, especially if they are linked
to your own relationships. You may be picking
up signals, both positive and negative, real
and unreal, but check out the truth before
you act. You could find that you have built an
embarrassing mountain out of a tiny molehill.

Venus in Scorpio or the 8th House

Values:
Self-control • Discretion • Honesty
Loyalty • Willpower

Occasionally:
Resentful • Secretive • Jealous
Vindictive • Calculating

In transit through Scorpio or the 8th House
You could spend this transit investigating
better rates of interest on your credit cards
but then again you could spend it behind
closed doors with your lover. Now, which is
the most appealing? If you are single, you
can still choose: look at a potential partner's
assets or utilizing your personal assets.
Any relationship that begins now could be
a long-term bet, so make it clear what you
expect and what you have to give.

Mars in Scorpio or the 8th House

Usually:
Relentless • Unflinching • Passionate
Controlled • Powerful

Occasionally:
Domineering • Callous • Cruel
Destructive • Controlling

In transit through Scorpio or the 8th House
Depending on what signals you are giving out,
this can be a time of incredible conflict or
amazing sex. With powerful underlying forces
at work, what you see may not be what you get.
During this transit any resentment or anger that
you have been stockpiling, especially toward
your closest partner, is bound to erupt. However,
if you are fundamentally happy, this could be a
time of intense emotional and physical sharing.

Sun in Sagittarius or the 9th House

November 23–December 21

Aims to be:
Broad-minded • Independent • Generous
Confident • Frank

Sometimes:
Inconsiderate • Irresponsible • Thoughtless
Overbearing • Arrogant

In transit through Sagittarius or the 9th House
You should be thinking big now rather than
concentrating on the detail. Take up any offers
to experience something brand new—you will
gain immense satisfaction from traveling abroad
or embarking on a course of study. The law,
publishing, and religion are all highlighted, so
if you are connected to these subjects take
advantage of an opportunity for growth or gain.

Moon in Sagittarius or the 9th House

Feelings are:
Visionary • Cheerful • Big-hearted
Philosophical • Optimistic

Occasionally:
Inconsistent • Extreme • Excessive
Careless • Inflated

In transit through Sagittarius or the 9th House

This transit works best at the weekend. The daily grind is just so boring—even the most diligent will find any excuse to evade responsibility right now. If you can't pack a bag and jump on a plane, try a good book or the movies—anything that plunges you headlong into a magical, inspirational and above all, different world. While the road of excess can occasionally lead to the palace of wisdom, try to avoid too much food or alcohol.

Venus in Sagittarius or the 9th House

Values:
Education • Freedom • Open-mindedness
Authenticity • Humor

Occasionally:
Flighty • Improvident • Extravagant
Blunt • Unfaithful

In transit through Sagittarius or the 9th House
This is a great time to go on holiday, and the
further away the better. Your outlook and
preconceptions are ready for new challenges,
and you'll get the most out of life if you open
your eyes and broaden your mind. It's likely that
you won't even have to make a special effort—
during this transit, you will naturally attract
friends and admirers from all walks of life who
can show you a new and entrancing world.

Mars in Sagittarius or the 9th House

Usually:
Jovial • Expansive • Enthusiastic
Versatile • Pioneering

Occasionally:
Slapdash • Rash • Unrestrained
Headstrong • Defiant

In transit through Sagittarius or the 9th House
Browbeating others with your recent discoveries won't win friends and influence people. You may feel enthralled, but those closest to you might be content to stay just as they are. Opening your mind to the great big world is no bad thing, however, and you could find that this is one of those brilliant "mini" turning points in life. But you must be astute enough to recognize then seize the opportunities that come your way.

Sun in Capricorn or the 10th House
December 22–January 20

Aims to be:
Constructive • Responsible • Single-minded
Dependable • Disciplined

Sometimes:
Self-centered • Exacting • Authoritative
Calculating • Judgmental

In transit through Capricorn or the 10th House
Take stock of your career. If you feel under-appreciated, now might be a good time to focus on why. Pinpoint any areas of dissatisfaction then see how they can be improved. If you find that there are more downs than ups in your current job, cast your net for a new opportunity. The chances are you will be noticed by an influential someone who can steer you in the right direction.

Moon in Capricorn or the 10th House

Feelings are:
Steady • Reserved • Sober
Serious • Cautious

Occasionally:
Gloomy • Depressive • Melancholy
Pessimistic • Cynical

In transit through Capricorn or the 10th House
This is a tricky transit to handle. In Capricorn, the Moon makes you fence off your feelings. Controlling your emotions will seem the easiest course of action as the general atmosphere may be a little gloomy and unreceptive. If the Moon is passing through your 10th House, you could be challenged about something close to your heart, leading to an uncharacteristic outburst. Put it down to experience, and don't let it upset you.

Venus in Capricorn or the 10th House

Values:
Self-sufficiency • Success • Dignity
Quality • Status

Occasionally:
Brooding • Aloof • Miserly
Snobbish • Pedantic

In transit through Capricorn or the 10th House
This is another transit when attention to grooming is essential—you'll find yourself in the limelight professionally as well as personally. Luckily, most of this attention is favorable, but there's no excuse for complacency. If you are looking to promote your cause or ask for a rise do it now, but remember to be tactful and show a little humility. The workplace is also ideal territory if you are looking for a little amorous action.

Mars in Capricorn or the 10th House

Usually:
Ambitious • Painstaking • Earnest
Successful • Sensual

Occasionally:
Manipulating • Wooden • Inconsiderate
Aloof • Unbending

In transit through Capricorn or the 10th House

Achievement is often one of Mars' main aims during this transit. Even the most laid-back may discover at least one unexpected or long-neglected goal demanding attention. While your confidence could be high, avoid a tendency toward arrogance, especially when dealing with authority figures in general and your boss in particular. Also, go easy on your colleagues at work if they don't keep pace with your ambition.

Sun in Aquarius or the 11th House

January 21–February 19

Aims to be:
Humane • Progressive • Thoughtful
Liberal • Individualistic

Sometimes:
Cold • Abstracted • Brusque
Tactless • Preoccupied

In transit through Aquarius or the 11th House
While cooperation is vital in friendships and other group involvements, it is important to maintain a sense of your individuality. During this period—in those brief moments when you are not socializing, campaigning or line dancing—you may find that you are continually redefining your place in society. Your goals have changed subtly over the last year, so some readjustment is appropriate.

Moon in Aquarius or the 11th House

Feelings are:
Truthful • Idealistic • Detached
Sincere • Loyal

Occasionally:
Irritable • Indifferent • Remote
Analytical • Impersonal

In transit through Aquarius or the 11th House
Look to your friends for emotional support if you
need it now, as they may understand you better
now than your partner or your family. Any recent
disagreements that have soured friendships will
benefit from a positive approach—so extend the
olive branch, even if it wasn't your fault. Projects
that involve working or socializing with others will
give great emotional satisfaction, and may help
you clarify your short- or long-term goals.

Venus in Aquarius or the 11th House

Values:
Friendship • Originality • Ingenuity
Objectivity • Intellect

Occasionally:
Unfeeling • Novelty-seeking • Indifferent
Perverse • Erratic

In transit through Aquarius or the 11th House
You are top of everyone's A-list now, and
certainly not in the mood for any quiet nights in.
Friends and colleagues seem to be involved
in all your undertakings, and the warm feelings
you have for them is reciprocated. Your closest
relationship may have to settle for second
place, so a few words of reassurance won't
go amiss. You may also find that you are
attracted to a worthy cause or project that
involves working with others.

Mars in Aquarius or the 11th House

Usually:
Unconventional • Independent • Inventive
Reforming • Unpredictable

Occasionally:
Rebellious • Stubborn • Abrupt
Inflexible • Impractical

In transit through Aquarius or the 11th House

As Mars passes through this House, you look
toward your future goals rather than the events
of the past. While you may want to get your
friends involved in your schemes and dreams,
they may find you a touch overpowering.
Resist the temptation to bludgeon them into
submission; instead, you may just let some
of your acquaintances wander adrift and
actively seek out more like-minded souls.

Sun in Pisces or the 12th House

February 20–March 20

Aims to be:
Easy-going • Flexible • Intuitive
Imaginative • Giving

Sometimes:
Confused • Manipulative • Weak-willed
Vague • Escapist

In transit through Pisces or the 12th House
This position completes your personal yearly cycle, ushering in a period of rest and recreation. Endings are emphasized now. How has your year been? Will you think of it as a special time, or has it been characterized by stressful relationships and a sense that you have no control over your life? If the latter is true, don't blame yourself. Solutions will appear if you allow them to.

Moon in Pisces or the 12th House

Feelings are:
Impressionable • Reflective • Fluid
Sensitive • Changeable

Occasionally:
Over-reactive • Hypochondriac • Weepy
Self-pitying • Dependent

In transit through Pisces or the 12th House
Your gut reaction will guide you best now. You are so in tune with the moods and feelings of others that you may actually shy away from socializing, preferring to contemplate in your own company. As with Moon transits through other water signs, the healing power of that magical element beckons. If the seaside isn't possible, a stroll around the nearest lake or pond could work wonders.

Venus in Pisces
or the 12th House

Values:
Spirituality • Generosity • Idealism
Imagination • Gentleness

Occasionally:
Unstable • Discontented • Indiscriminate
Unfocussed • Fantasizing

In transit through Pisces or the 12th House
A classic transit for romantic triangles, this
can also be a time when, no matter how
careful you are, you are liable to get caught.
Any new relationship requires objectivity, no
matter how fabulous the prospects. Before
you open your heart, make sure they are free
to love you. Positively, you are the epitome
of selflessness and you can devote yourself
to others' wellbeing. Negatively, watch your
valuables now.

Mars in Pisces
or the 12th House

Usually:
Subtle • Self-sacrificing • Unselfish
Compassionate • Ingenious

Occasionally:
Unrealistic • Chaotic • Devious
Deceptive • Evasive

In transit through Pisces or the 12th House
It is difficult for Mars to operate effectively here
and you may find that you feel vaguely irritated
for much of the time. You'll benefit most if you
use your skills and energy to help others rather
than for purely selfish reasons. There may be
some surprises as well and, while secret affairs
can be initiated now, it may be revealed that
someone is not all they pretend to be. Watch
and wait before making any serious moves!

Index